JAMES MAPES'

# THE WORKBOOK

## The Magic of Quantum Leap Thinking

# JAMES MAPES'

# THE WORKBOOK

## The Magic of Quantum Leap Thinking

Library of Congress Catalog Card Number 95-94283

ISBN 0-9645442-0-2


Manufactured in the United States of America
First Printing 1995



Published by
*THE QUANTUM LEAP THINKING ORGANIZATION*
Wilton, CT



Produced by
*PPC BOOKS*
Westport, CT

# ACKNOWLEDGMENTS

I would like to express my special appreciation to Sherri Daley. Without her tireless work and dedication in assembling and editing, this workbook would not have been possible.

Special thanks are due to those friends who patiently reviewed the manuscript: Susan Granger, Ken Williams and Donald P. Granger.

I would like to thank Robert Delezenne for his wonderful illustrations.

And finally, I want to thank all those who have influenced my own growth process throughout the years, especially my grandfather, Samuel James, for being who he was.

# TABLE OF CONTENTS

# INTRODUCTION

For many years, people have requested supportive material following my presentations. With gentle persuasion and encouragement by good friends, I have compiled the basis of what I believe to be the most important elements of Quantum Leap Thinking.

The premise of this workbook is simple: By changing the way you think, you will discover solutions to personal and professional challenges. You will learn to overcome self-limiting beliefs which may stand in the way of your growth and fulfillment.

The information, exercises, strategies and distinctions in this workbook are designed to assist you in examining and questioning your beliefs and perceptions - and to create positive change and magic in your life.

Let the journey begin ...

# JAMES MAPES'

# THE WORKBOOK

## The Magic of Quantum Leap Thinking

PART ONE:

# THE
# FOUNDATION

**W**ebster's Dictionary defines magic as *"... the art that purports to control or forecast natural events or forces by invoking the supernatural; a sleight of hand or conjuring for entertainment; a mysterious quality of enchantment."*

In my opinion, none of that is magic.

> **A quantum leap, no matter how infinitesimal, always makes a sharp break with the past. It is the discontinuous jump of an electron from one orbit to another, with the particle mysteriously leaving no trace of its path. It is the instantaneous collapse of a wave of probabilities into a single real event.**
>
> **It is the link between two entirely separate locations, events or ideas, that magical moment when the previously inexplicable is suddenly explained, and a radical new theory is born.**
>
> **— *Science Digest***

Now, that's magic. When scientists begin to use the words "mysterious" and "magical" to explain phenomena in physics, I know the concept has finally arrived.

For thousands of years, magic has been an integral part of many cultures. Only in the past decade has the Western world begun to accept it as part of the real world. Werner Heisenberg acknowledged it when he demonstrated that observing an atom affected the properties of the atoms themselves. According to the Heisenberg Theory of Uncertainty, both the momentum and the position of an atom are *potentially* present in nature, but not *actually* present until the attempt is made to measure them. Then either the wave length (momentum) side of the atoms or the particle (location) side appears.

The universe is made up of facts and their opposites. We are usually not aware of the paradoxical nature of things because we cannot see both sides at once. For example, a cube can be seen from several different perspectives.

At first glance, you may be looking at the cube from above. When you shift your perspective, you see the cube from below. And yet, with another shift of perspective, you can see the cube with one side prominent. If you have trouble, try coloring in one side. Then, on the cube below, color in a different side.

Just like the atom's invisible components, the paradoxical cube shifts its shape and perspective, but nothing really changed, did it? Just the way you looked at it. By a single choice of observation, the cube's perspective is fixed and all other possibilities become invisible.

Doctors have found that the power of the mind performs apparent miracles, too. Among the critically and terminally ill, patients with good attitudes fared better than patients who were convinced they were going to die. Professional athletics coaches admitted that *imagining* a successfully executed golf swing (tackle, basketball free shot, etc.) improved performance as much or more than actual, physical practice.

Red phosphorous and potassium chlorate are stable chemicals when kept in isolation; but when they are mixed together and shaken, they explode. There is undeniable energy, and a transformation takes place.

That is magic. And we have the power to create magic like that ourselves. We can create that magical moment when the previously inexplicable is suddenly explained, and a radical new theory is born. That moment is a quantum leap, and Quantum Leap Thinking is the process that can get us there.

The skills that comprise the process are the chemicals which together create an undeniable energy, and a strategy for personal and professional success takes form. When you incorporate this strategy in your daily life and practice it with commitment, you will experience your own explosion.

Quantum Leap Thinking cannot be explained in typical linear fashion because the concepts, like a group of chemicals mixed and interacting together, work in harmony.

The Quantum Leap process begins with a three-dimensional triangle, base down, on which is balanced a three-dimensional rectangle comprised of 14 sections. These are the **14 Points of Quantum Leap Thinking** which spin like a top, perfectly balanced on the point of the triangle.

The three sides of the triangle on which everything else is built are three foundation skills: creative thinking, managing change, and continuous learning. The foundation must be in place and meticulously maintained before the top can spin.

## Foundation Skill #1:

# *CREATIVE THINKING*

**C**hildren are highly creative, but then comes the process of education and conditioning. Most of us have been taught that the part of our brains measured by IQ and aptitude tests is the key factor to getting ahead. Our educational system rewards those who are smart and discourages those who are not, and we carry with us that history of success and failure. We identify with that which discourages us from expressing our natural creativity. In a sense, we become stuck in what we've learned and blind to our own creative natures.

Our creative side gets ignored. Many of us still believe that intelligence alone should be able to solve problems in both our personal and business relationships. This "intelligence trap" has led many of us to believe that innovation, problem-solving, productivity and open communication can be handled by logic. Creative growth is suppressed or, worse yet, punished. The result is often frustration, confusion, guilt, blame and anxiety.

Logic has its place; it's necessary. But creative thinking and logical thinking should be considered two sides of the same coin. The creative side of our nature includes intuition, ideas, dreams, and fantasy. Without ideas and dreams, intelligence is a rather useless tool. The balance between the two is the mark of peak performers.

Curiously, the majority of people hesitate to recognize the breakthroughs in their own lives as creative acts. If I ask an audience to name people they view as creative, they invariably list famous artists, writers, musicians or inventors. No one has ever said, "Me."

To make matters worse, our creative side is elusive and delicate; it needs constant nurturing and trust. Fear, excessive effort, criticism, and lack of freedom and space can send the creative self into hiding. But there is a tremendous payoff to recognizing, believing in and paying attention to our creative side. If physicists can "create" one or the other of an atom's properties by simply changing their perspective, we can "create" things in our own lives, too. The invisible can be made visible; the impossible, possible. Let me give you just five pieces of creative advice.

## Creative Advice #1: Create space.

Pretend you have a date book in which every moment is filled. In order to stay on schedule, you must rush from one event to another. There is little opportunity for something new, spontaneous, interesting or creative. There is simply no space on the agenda for creative possibilities unless you include space as part of the agenda.

Create stop time. Make the space to be alone. Give yourself the gift of time alone or demand it of yourself. Make it a priority. Learn a relaxation exercise, walk in the woods, or just sit quietly. Stop. If every minute of every waking hour is scheduled with obligations, deadlines and activity, there is no room for anything else.

I know you can find reasons for being so busy, but think of your life as a full glass of water. The only way you can have room for fresh water is to pour some water out.

Space and stop time do not have to be meditative or reclusive, although some people may make that choice. Your stop time should fit your life-style: jogging, sitting in a sauna, listening to music, walking on the beach, lying in a hammock, ironing, doing your nails, getting a facial. You can take twenty minutes a day or one day a week. If your significant other is tolerant and supportive, take a week for yourself every six months. Demanding "alone time" enables you to become more creative.

Being busy does not necessarily mean being productive. Busy-ness is often an unconscious choice to avoid looking within yourself.

Introspection can be uncomfortable, but it's part of the creative process.

### Creative Advice #2: Do something different.

Breaking your routine is mandatory for the creative process. It doesn't have to be dramatic or dangerous. You might do something you think you wouldn't enjoy or something you suspect would make you uneasy. Go to the opera if you gravitate towards sports. Go to a ball game if you usually go to the theatre. Read a biography if you always read fiction, or poetry if you only read the newspaper. Or you could go fly a kite. Find a way to break your old ways and shift your patterns of behavior.

Choose to drive a different route to work, eat a different type of food. Go rafting. Go fishing. Walk in a mall. Consciously break your usual, comfortable routine.

### Creative Advice #3: Challenge assumptions.

Most of us have been taught since early childhood to respect authority. We were taught to color within the lines, write neatly on the line, and above all, be careful not to cross the line. What line?

If we're not diligent, we fall victim to our ingrained habits of living in a space where the barriers to achievement have become our own justified, accepted circumstances.

Look at the drawing below:

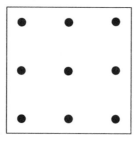

Connect the nine dots together with four straight lines without removing your pencil or pen from the paper. Give yourself two or three minutes. Then look at the next page for the solution.

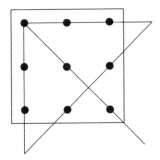

If you assumed that your line had to stay within the box, your assumption stopped your creative process.

Think of that box as your circumstances, your life, what you "know" to be true. In order to solve that puzzle, you had step outside what you believe. You had to "think outside the box."

That has become a common catch phrase, but few people really understand it or put it into action. Assumptions box us in. Assumptions box in our creativity.

Now see if you can make the number 6 out of Roman numeral 9. Take your time; be creative.

People have done everything from cutting the number in half horizontally and holding it in front of a mirror to struggling with complicated mathematical equations, but the easiest solution is to simply write an **S** in front of it. Did you think of that? Maybe you assumed that you could not add to it, but I didn't give you any rules. How many possibilities and opportunities do you miss because you have made an assumption?

Assumptions get in the way of successful personal and professional relationships. Think how damaging the following assumptions could be during business negotiations, a marital argument, or a disciplinary discussion with a child.

1) Assuming the other person values the same things you do.

2) Assuming you know what is expected of you.

3) Assuming others know what you want of them.

4) Assuming your way is the right way and the only way.

5) Assuming others' understanding of a term or word is the same as your understanding (i.e. quality, customer service, empowerment, love, selfish, commitment).

6) Assuming things will never change or *should* never change.

7) Assuming you know what makes someone else feel loved by knowing what makes you feel loved.

8) Assuming that everyone's rules for friendship or relationship are the same as your rules for friendship or relationship.

9) Assuming you are powerless and cannot make a difference, or worse yet, assuming that you have complete power over others.

10) Assuming something must be done a certain way because that's the way it has always been done.

Making assumptions is arrogant. You have assumed you know more than the other person, the situation, or the circumstance. You are assuming that you are in complete control. The arrogance of assumption is sometimes destructive, but it always gets in the way of the creative process.

Take five minutes and list fifteen things that you know to be true about your children, spouse, friends, relationships, government, your talents or your business.

1._____

2._____

3._____

4._____

5._____

6._____

7._____

8._____

9._____

10._____

11._____

12._____

13._____

14._____

15._____

Now read them over and pretend that none of them are true. Does that change things? What possibilities are open to you now?

_____

_____

_____

_____

_____

If we can put aside our own assumptions and think outside the box, we are open to diversity. If we can challenge the assumptions of others, we are open to possibility.

It takes great courage and massive support to think outside the box and venture into unknown territory. It also takes a conscious choice to accept the premise that our circumstances are self-created; they have become so familiar that we have accepted them as real. Our ability to be creative becomes blocked when we assume that our circumstances will never change. For many, unfortunately, it is more comfortable to feel powerless than to challenge the system. It is change we seek and change we resist, the ultimate human paradox.

## Creative Advice #4: Create continuous challenges.

There is nothing worse than boredom. It causes accidents in the workplace, inattention in the classroom, and disaster at home. It takes work and commitment to create challenge, because boredom is comfortable; but remember that boredom breeds complacency, and complacency goes nowhere. To foster creativity, you need to drum up continuous renewal.

That may mean joining a discussion group, signing up for learning adventures like Outward Bound, taking workshops, listening to tapes or reading books which support the energy and courage necessary to challenge yourself and others.

## Creative Advice #5: Forgive failure.

When an idea is generated, we have to test it. It might work, and it might not. Failure is a by-product of creativity.

Creativity is not necessarily about getting things right. The creative spirit explodes when you take risks, make mistakes and learn. Children don't need to take lessons in walking, talking or exploring. They try, fail, and try again until they get it right. The learning process revolves around failure.

No set of automatons is as valuable as one creative individual, but creative individuals are often dismissed as eccentrics, or denigrated as rebellious showoffs. However, these oddballs often discover cures for disease, invent the micro-chip or come up with an amazing marketing campaign. It's only after these mavericks produce a positive result that they become valuable and tolerated. In an era of incomprehensible change, these are precisely the people who will become an even more valuable asset. They desperately need the luxury of making a few mistakes along the way. Creativity needs space and freedom.

You may have the heart to forgive others their mistakes, but just as important is forgiving yourself. Reread the above and consider yourself one of those creative oddballs who just might change the world. Then treat yourself accordingly.

Foundation Skill #2:

# MANAGING CHANGE

**A**s creative, learning individuals, we may crave challenge, but unfortunately, as human beings, we have a natural resistance to it. Because of that, most change is thrust upon us. In order to handle these unwanted intrusions, it helps to understand the nature of the process itself.

**There are essentially three types of change.**

1. <u>Crisis change</u> is forced on us. We react to some catastrophic event or personal upset. It can be as dramatic as the death of a loved one or as mundane as a job promotion, but crisis change triggers a reactive response. We are momentarily unsettled, but as soon as we are able, we set out to manage the changes the crisis created.

2. If we wait long enough, <u>evolutionary change</u> will occur. We notice everyone else is changing and we think it would be a good idea if we followed suit, or we think we have to in order to survive. Evolutionary change subverts personal choice and often results in feeling victimized. It is as uncontrollable as crisis change and more insidious because it happens slowly and gives the illusion that we are in control.

3. Visionary change is pro-active. We create it; we cause it. Visionary change is learning, anticipating and realizing a vision. The vision provides us with the tension or energy needed to create and manage the unavoidable changes. No matter how much change takes place, the power of the vision provides us with a center to which we can always return for renewal.

It will help to understand the chronological stages of the change process, too.

1. **Resistance.** We resist with a slew of responses: denial, despair, anger, blame, violence, or sickness. All change creates loss. We may lose a loved one, our home, simple security or familiarity with our daily tasks. Whatever that imminent loss is, we fight to keep it. We resist the change that threatens our security.

2. **The Dead Zone.** Resistance begins to fade, but we are not yet ready to embrace change. This is a time of re-orientation. Often we feel at our worst; we're lost. We feel a combination of hope and despair, confusion and adjustment. We search for meaning in the change.

3. **The Leap.** We've resisted, acknowledged our losses, and experienced the dead zone. Now we're ready to embrace the change. Once we do that, there is renewed energy and a feeling of control. We have purpose and direction. We have survived that change.

Whether the change is caused by crisis, evolution, or your own vision, there are specific action steps to successfully manage the change process.

**Be Aware.** Pay close attention to what's going on around you. You will inevitably encounter resistance. Change of any kind affects the entire structure of a system beyond our immediate selves. Even those who love you may undermine your decision to make a change.

Pay attention to your own patterns of behavior. Recognize the warning signs of stress, tell yourself the truth, and keep pushing forward, gently.

**Accept Compromise.** You must be willing to take one step back for every two steps forward. You want long-term change, not a bunch of quick fixes, so you have to negotiate with yourself. Change is painful, and pain can stop you in your tracks or keep you razor-sharp and alert. Commitment, resilience and persistence. All meaningful long-term change takes time.

**Weigh the Pros and Cons.** Draw a line down the center of a piece of paper. On the left side, list all the benefits of the change; on the right, list the negatives. Be honest and you will intuitively know in what direction to proceed.

**Make a Contract.** Tell somebody. Verbalize your commitment. Then write a contract stating exactly what change you intend to make and set a deadline for yourself. By entering into a written contract and declaring yourself to someone who can serve as a compassionate observer or coach, you empower others to empower you.

**Break the Change into Small Steps.** Divide the process into small parts, each with a specific written statement, a goal, and deadline date. What doesn't get measured, doesn't get done. Set your priorities with the easiest task first. Once you take that first successful step to action, you're on your way.

**Orchestrate Reality.** People say, "I'll believe it when I see it." The truth is we see it when we believe it. You have to create a belief before the change can happen. You must pretend. See it. Breathe it. Sense it. Feel it as if it had already taken place. Your subconscious is a powerful tool.

You can orchestrate reality for those around you, too.
- Develop and communicate a critical mass of information.
- Respect others' values, concerns and fears.
- Create energy. Create the tension that the change will resolve.
- Allow those involved to participate and retain control.

In other words, make it real for them, too. Educate, empower, and lead them to see the same reality you do.

**Create a Routine.** Set a routine and stick to it, no matter what. Routine becomes rote; routine makes things stick. And routine is comfortable at a time when you will crave comfort most.

**Be Patient.** It takes at least thirty days of practice to etch a new groove into your pattern. Some of us become anxious; and after giving the process what we consider an appropriate amount of time, we revert to our old ways. Patience is the choice of winners.

**See the Big Picture.** Recognize and accept that change is unsettling and awkward, not only for you, but also for those around you. Any change affects the system as a whole. When you can see the whole picture, your ability to support others increases with your awareness.

**Develop a Support System.** Be prepared. Any major change can cause severe depression brought about by fear. Develop a support system of friends, family or co-workers. Support gives the space necessary to allow expression of the discomfort and pain which accompanies change. Support provides a center of safety. Support creates stability.

The totally independent person may look brave, but he or she is cut off from others and doesn't have the benefit of strength in numbers. An over-dependent person often clings to dead-end situations or destructive relationships. Strike a balance. Become interdependent; join forces. Interdependence does not mean giving up freedom or identity; interdependence means being willing to both give and ask for support.

**Be Creative.** Change demands a consistent flow of innovative ideas. Be creative yourself and work to support a creative environment for those around you.

**Develop Superb Communication Skills.** Increase the flow of communication. Make a point of talking every day to the people around you. Touch base consistently. When people know you're there for them, they can face difficult changes; and the same holds true for you. Bring the family together for meetings or at least have dinner together. Take your department out to lunch at unexpected times. Communication must be visible for change to take hold.

Dissent is necessary and healthy. It's part of the communication process, too. Encourage criticism and open dialogue. Let people voice their resistance.

Do your best to give positive feedback. Change creates fear. People need to be acknowledged for making a contribution, no matter how small. The big picture is made up of many small brush strokes. Success comes one small step at a time. Failure doesn't exist; only learning exists. Make the feedback positive and empowering.

Listen, ask questions, and empathize. People seldom want to be cheered up; they want to be heard and understood. Set aside your own need to be right and simply listen. Paraphrase what the other person says, so he or she knows you understand. You will help create behavioral transformations beyond your wildest dreams. You will allow people to release pent-up, fear-based emotions.

**Celebrate.** Celebration is completion. Celebration is validation. Have a party. Have a glass of champagne or go to the movies. Reward yourself for completing small steps along the way, and celebrate handsomely when you've managed the change completely.

Foundation Skill #3:

# *CONTINUOUS LEARNING*

## THE CIRCLE OF LEARNING

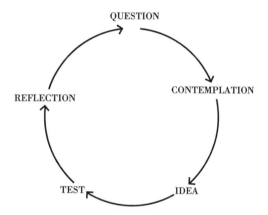

QUESTION

CONTEMPLATION

IDEA

TEST

REFLECTION

**S**ome of us get stuck in the question mode and never get any further. We quit once we get an acceptable answer. Learning stops right there because there is no contemplation.

Contemplation is the space for creativity and the opportunity for ideas. This is where ideas are born; but even there, we can get stopped if we accept the idea as fact and don't ask more questions. Worse yet, someone else's ideas can be taught as fact without allowing the possibility of another point of view.

Once we get into the idea stage, we might get excited with ourselves, but we can't stop here, either. The circle is in constant motion. It takes real courage to test that idea out in the real world. It may work and it may not, and success is sometimes as scary and difficult as failure.

The stage of reflection is comfortable, too. We might think that is a

**15**

great place to stay for a while, but if we become complacent, too comfortable with our ideas, the Circle of Learning grinds to a halt. It is not easy to keep the Circle in continuous motion.

If we are in charge of creating our own destiny, education and training, then the purpose of the Circle of Learning is the most important investment we can make in shaping that destiny. Learning must be pro-active.

Learning how to learn is a real processsss. A question is asked and the process is put in motion: question, contemplation, idea, test and reflection.

# THE TRINITY FOR LEARNING

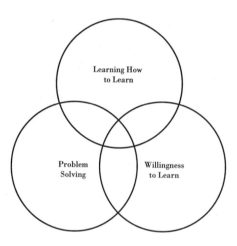

Problem-solving seems to be the easiest part of the trinity to understand. Solving problems is what most of us remember best about our formal education. But problem-solving is not the part of the learning process which willcreate the most magic in your life.

Willingness to learn affords the potential for personal mastery. Willingness to learn presupposes a desire and a commitment to step into the unknown. It requires the understanding and acceptance that learning is never-ending, on-going process in the creation and achievement of your vision. It requires a commitment to experiencing your life to the fullest, day-by-day, moment-by-moment.

1. Learning is solving your own problems for your own reasons.

2. Learning is knowing more than just prescribed answers; it is developing a foundation for answers based on your curiosity.

3. Learning is more than studying or being trained. Learning is a way of thinking about life.

4. Learning is a starting point and does not have an end point. Learning is on-going, a habit, a process.

5. Learning is a methodology which requires thought, courage, energy, commitment and support.

When we are unaware of our own personal power to change, stretch and grow, we believe we are powerless; that people, things or situations are doing it to us. But a new reality is available to us if we can see all the choices available and make the most empowering choices possible.

Quantum Leap Thinking is the process through which we can create that new reality. With the strong base of creative thinking, effectively managing change, and continuous learning, we are ready for the 14 points which complete the explosion.

Take the leap.

PART TWO:

# THE 14 POINTS OF QUANTUM LEAP THINKING

## Point # 1

# *PAY ATTENTION*

**M**y suitcase disappeared on one of my trips recently. It just failed to show up. I stood there in the baggage claim area stupidly watching everybody else's luggage for a long time before I finally admitted it was lost and told the airline people. I filled out some forms in triplicate.

I was told it would certainly be on the next flight, but it wasn't. It didn't arrive before I went to bed, and it didn't arrive during the night, and nobody came bouncing over at breakfast to tell me that it had been delivered at dawn.

I was not happy. All the assurances I received from the airline personnel did very little to calm the storm in my mind. I felt helpless and out of control. There was absolutely nothing I could do. After breakfast, I left stern messages for the airline people at the hotel's front desk, and stormed out to take a walk. It was a beautiful vibrant spring morning in Scottsdale, Arizona. The air smelled wonderful; the spring flowers were in bloom, and the gardens and lawns were gloriously green. But I went to war with myself. "What if my suitcase had disappeared into some airline black hole? What about my new shirts? My favorite shoes could never be replaced. Why didn't I bring a travel kit in my carry-on bag? How could I have been so stupid?" I had left five pages of notes for a chapter of my book in my suitcase, and I had nothing to wear for my presentation.

Suddenly I realized I had walked four long blocks. I was angry. I had disappeared from the beautiful spring day and deliberately walked into a dark little pit of irritating misery.

I looked around. I smelled the spring flowers and felt the sun warming my face. A mama duck followed by eight tiny babies swam by in a sun-drenched pond. I smiled. I was, miraculously, happy. The worst that could happen, I decided, was that I had to buy some new clothes.

On the way back to the hotel, I remembered a Zen story about a middle-aged man who had fought his way up the corporate ladder. On the way, his marriage fell apart; he was estranged from his children, bored with his money, and physically sick.

Then someone told him there was a wise man who knew three secrets to a happy life. The man instantly quit his job, sold his home and began the quest to find the wise man with the secrets of happiness.

He traveled throughout the world, enduring many hardships, but at last he was rewarded. He found the wise man sequestered high on a mountain, and knelt before him. "I have traveled a long way and endured many hardships, Master," he said. "Please tell me the three secrets of a happy life."

"Most certainly," replied the master. "The first secret of life is to pay attention."

The man was delirious. He could most certainly do that! "And what else, Master?" he begged.

"The second secret of life," said the wise Zen master, "is to pay attention."

The man could scarcely believe his ears. But the wise old master made it even clearer. He closed his eyes and said, "And the third secret of life, young man, is to pay attention."

Most people never really pay attention. I was certainly not paying attention on my walk in Scottsdale. To pay attention you must be in the moment, not in your mind. I needed to be in that beautiful spring day, not in the nasty pit of my lost luggage.

Fritz Pearls, the great pioneer of gestalt therapy, said that most anxiety and stress is caused by "... living in a dead past or an unborn future." Guilt from the past. Fear of the future.

Healing, however, is in the present.

When you began to understand the importance and practice of being in the present, life suddenly takes on a whole new dimension. Appreciation, joy, ecstasy and healing are the payoffs.

Read the sentence in the triangle shown below:

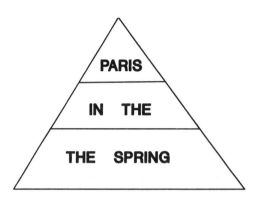

What did you read? If you are like the majority of people, you read "Paris in the spring." If so, read it again, and this time, pay attention. The sentence reads, "Paris in the *the* spring."

If you saw the extra "the", congratulations. You were paying attention. Try it out on your friends and family. You will discover that most people miss the second "the". Why? Because we are conditioned to see what we expect to see, or what we want to see. The mind will try to make sense out of non-sense. Sometimes it works to our benefit, and sometimes it doesn't. Sometimes we don't see something which is very important.

Invisible opportunities surround us all the time. In order to see them,

we have to pay attention. It is the skill with which we can develop awareness, and without which there can be no quantum leaps at all.


## DEVELOPING THE SKILL

### Exercise #1: Pay attention to your body.

Make yourself comfortable. Close your eyes and listen to the beating of your heart. Become aware of the physical sensations taking place in your body: your breathing, the temperature of your skin, the pressure of your body against the furniture. Listen to your thoughts, your mind-chatter. Do you think the exercise is silly? Are you tired? Notice the thoughts that come and go in your head.

As you become aware of each thought, let it go. It may help to imagine your thought process as a series of video clips. Observe, let go, and see what other clips emerge. Continue the exercise for five minutes. If you feel restless, acknowledge it, let it go and objectively observe the next feeling or judgment.

### Exercise #2: Pay attention to your surroundings.

Look around. Take your time. Look at a tree. See the different hues of the colors which make up the leaves. Observe a flower. Notice the variety of tones and shades of the petals. What's moving? Clouds, butterflies, birds, animals, the branches of a tree? Give your full attention to each subject you choose to observe for one minute. If your mind-chatter interferes, notice it, and then refocus your attention.

After ten minutes, close your eyes and become aware of the sounds around you: the sound of the wind, the ticking of a clock, the hum of the refrigerator. Further off there might be the sound of an airplane, the distant buzz of traffic, a phone ringing, a squirrel chattering, a crow shrieking, a sparrow singing. For ten minutes, allow nothing else to exist except sound. Become the sound.

### Exercise #3: Pay attention to what you touch.

Take your favorite piece of fruit, a strawberry, an orange, grapes, or an apple. Observe the color. Feel the texture. Smell the skin. Peel it or cut it open, and observe the change in color and texture on the inside.

Hear the sound as you slice it. Watch as you slowly move the fruit up to your mouth. Take a bite. Savor the flavor. Nothing else exists. Allow yourself five minutes to do the exercise.

**Exercise #4: Pay attention to what you see.**

Light a candle and watch the flame. Watch how it flickers and changes color. See if you can keep your focus on the flame of the candle for ten minutes. If your attention drifts away, gently bring it back to the flame.

These exercises are meant to help you break the habit of being distracted. We don't see things or hear things, sometimes very important things, because we are unconscious of the "now." We forget to seize the moment, and so the moment gets away.

Most people learn to scuba dive because they want to experience the incredible mysteries of underwater sea life. It is a silent and secretive world, eerily suspended, its inhabitants cleverly camouflaged or unabashedly brilliant. And yet I have seen divers speed through the depths, missing the very thing for which they were searching. They blast around looking for some preconceived fantasy instead of paying attention to the beauty of what they're swimming past: a bright piece of coral, a sea fan, a delicate sea anemone, or a cluster of small fish. Suddenly the dive is over and they are full of disappointment and complaints.

A fellow diver and I approach diving a different way. We developed a course called "The Zen of Diving." A Zen diver will first achieve neutral buoyancy, hanging limp and motionless, face down in the water. Then he focuses his attention on three or four square feet of ocean floor.

At first, the area may look like a lifeless piece of sand or rock, but as the diver stares, a whole world begins to open up. The sand shifts, the smallest of sea creatures emerge, colors change, and what at first appeared to be empty and lifeless becomes an absorbing, vibrant world of activity.

The "Zen of Diving" serves as a perfect metaphor for a successful approach to life. Whether you are a manager in a large corporation, a member of an office support staff, a homemaker, or an independent entrepreneur, everything becomes alive when you focus on it.

Once you've slowed down, you can pay attention:

1.... to your emotions.

Your ability to be in touch with your emotions gives you direction to make the decisions necessary to enhance your emotional well-being.

2.... to your body.

Your body is continually sending signals: when you're hungry, when you're tired, when you're scared, and when you're doing the right thing.

3.... to your thoughts.

Your thoughts precede your actions. You may not think so, but you have control over what you think. When you learn to listen to yourself, you will recognize negative thoughts like shame and guilt; and you can change judgment into curiosity, criticism into suggestions, and guilt into understanding.

4.... to what's around you.

When you pay attention to your surroundings, you enjoy it more. Your internal clock slows down; you become focused. Your natural creativity has time to be unleased, and opportunities magically appear.

5.... to what you're doing.

Break your old habits and develop new ways of thinking and

new ways of behaving. You need to recognize when you are operating out of fear so you can make that fear work for you, turn it into power. But habits are unconscious. To break out of old patterns, first we have to know they're there.

6.... to what you want and need.

You can set goals only when you know what you want. Make two lists: What do you <u>want</u>? What do you <u>need</u>?

7.... to others.

Most people are so eager to get across their point of view that they forget to listen to others. They don't know that in order to be heard, they must first listen.

    a. Set aside your ego.

Give up that part of you that believes what you're more important than the other guy. Set aside your need to dominate the conversation. Your own voice is your biggest block to listening.

    b. Suspend judgment.

Your opinions will only get in the way. Allow the other person to be right. You can't hear him otherwise.

    c. Listen with your whole being.

<u>Feel</u> what the other person is saying. Your intuition may prove invaluable. Focus on body language, breathing patterns, tone of voice, and speed of speech. Words are important, but sometimes they get in the way.

d. Never interrupt.

The fastest way to lose rapport is to interrupt. It kills communication. If you think of something to say while you are listening, make a mental note or jot it down. Before you make judgments, rebuttals or comparisons, be sure you have heard the other person through.

e. Ask for details.

If the language you hear is too technical or unfamiliar, listen until the person is finished and then ask for clarification, definitions or explanations. Repeat it to be sure you are both in agreement before proceeding with your conversation.

f. Use the word "and."

"And" is one of your most powerful communication tools. It validates the other person. "But" or "however" are killers. Listen to what the person has just said and respond, "I understand your point of view, and I think this."

g. Be patient.

Foot tapping, looking off into the distance, pencil-tapping and finger-drumming signal that you are not listening. If you are nervous, calm yourself with a relaxation exercise before meeting with the person. Only a calm mind can be open to listening.

If there is one point of the Fourteen Points of Quantum Leap Thinking more important than all the rest, it is **Pay Attention**. None of the others can happen for you until you first pay attention to what you're doing, where you're going, why and with whom.

# QUANTUM LEAP THINKPOINTS

Invisible opportunities surround us all the time.

Healing is in the present.

Everything becomes alive when you focus on it.

You have control over what you think.

"And" is your most powerful communication tool.

Your opinions will only get in the way.

The secret to increasing the quality of life is to pay attention.

## YOUR TURN

Everything I tell you in this workbook means nothing unless you take the time to apply it to your own life. Sometimes the relevance is easy to see; other times, it may take some doing. In either case, it will help to make some notes about yourself.

That is what **YOUR TURN** is all about. I've done my part. Now it's your turn.

# YOUR TURN

Take one day and make a commitment to PAY ATTENTION from the moment you open your eyes until the time you fall asleep.

**Consciously** do the following:

Slow down

Focus

Be patient

Suspend judgment

Listen

**Choose** three moments during the day to pay attention to your body, to what's around you, your emotions and your thoughts and **write** four sentences describing each moment. Choose moments that otherwise may have gone unnoticed—opening the curtains, your first cup of coffee or tea, or that last-minute good-bye hug from your spouse or child.

Be specific. Center your attention on the little things: the way the blankets smell in the morning before you get out of bed, the tick of the clock, the angle of the sun through a window, or the temperature of the air. Remember you can CHOOSE what to focus on. You control your thoughts. Pay attention.

Moment #1:

1. _____
2. _____
3. _____
4. _____

Moment #2:

1. _____
2 _____
3. _____
4. _____

Moment #3:

1. _____
2. _____
3. _____
4. _____

Point #2

# *TURN FEAR INTO POWER*

**F**ear does not actually exist; it is an illusion, nothing more than **F**alse **E**vidence **A**ppearing **R**eal. You project your fears out in the world; then you accumulate the necessary evidence to prove them to be true. Fear feels real, looks real, and you can back it up with facts. You see what you believe, and what you see becomes proof. You have imagined it, and your own imagination is the source and the power of fear.

Fear has its place. In the proper circumstances, fear may save our lives. In the deepest recesses of our genes still lingers the echo of basic survival. The problem is that many of us still unconsciously respond from the primitive fight-or-flight mechanism which once served us so well. Lions and tigers and bears take on different personalities. We interpret minor annoyances as threats to survival and act accordingly.

Fear isn't necessarily destructive, either. Fear can be invigorating and motivating. Famous actors, sports figures, artists, dancers, salespeople and public speakers often admit they have butterflies before they go on stage, enter a contest or approach a prospective client. Many of them say they would feel lost without that delicious tingle of fear. The feeling gives them energy and focus.

As long as you continue to grow, you will always be afraid, because fear is a natural part of the growth process. Instead of wasting our energies being careful to avoid discomfort and fear, we need to accept fear as a partner. This is a major paradigm shift for the majority of us. You are not alone.

Our fears grow from an elemental fear of loss: loss of control, love, esteem, or health. I view the fear of loss as the center of a wheel to which are attached the spokes of secondary fears.

### 1. Fear of Rejection

Fear of rejection jeopardizes our self-esteem and our sense of being loved. It triggers a self-protective mechanism. It doesn't matter if we are making love, working, or partying. Unconsciously, we withdraw from battle. We rationalize that if we don't put ourselves in the position of being turned down, we can avoid rejection. Unfortunately, when we avoid confrontations, the fear becomes the reality: we are isolated

and victimized.

Fear of rejection can also manipulate us to be aggressive, controlling, possessive, or jealous, and our logical mind tells us our behavior is justified. If we control those around us, they can't reject us. If we are possessive or jealous, we can hold on to the people we love. The result, however, is that people feel trapped or intimidated. They go away, if they can, because we push them away. We created rejection when what we wanted most was acceptance.

Criticism is a sensitive issue even when our self-esteem is rock-solid, but when the fear of rejection colors communication, even constructive criticism can be deadly. The threat of criticism can manipulate us to wear the "right" clothes, drive the "right" vehicle, and be seen in the "right" places. We may even sabotage our own integrity. Fear of rejection gives criticism the power to rob us of self-esteem, imagination, creativity and desire.

### 2. Fear of Change

All change, positive or negative, involves giving up something, real or imagined, so we must confront our basic terror of loss whenever we face a change in our lives. To make matters worse, it is basic human nature to resist change: our bodies, our brains and our behavior have a built-in penchant to stay the same. We lose a part of our own self-definition when we experience change. The fear of change is elemental, practically a foundation for understanding all the other secondary fears.

### 3. Fear of Success

Fear of success is intriguing. We *want* to be successful, but we seem to set up our own stumbling blocks. Success is too much work, too much responsibility. Success demands sacrifice. These things may be true, but the real resistance is caused by this: Success is change.

Believe it or not, lack of success often creates a secret sense of relief. We like the status quo. We have adjusted to it, even if it is ugly. It is part of us. We may live in "tolerable discomfort," an unhappy situation, but we created it, and it has become easy and familiar.

### 4. Fear of Failure.

It's natural to be afraid of failing when you start a new business, get promoted, begin a new relationship, prospect for new clients, ask for help, learn to ski, talk to an angry customer, present a new idea to the boss or tell the truth.

Our childhood experiences have a great deal of influence on how we deal with this fear. If, at home or school, we were threatened with humiliation or punishment for failing, the fear of the punishment prevents us, as adults, from taking the risks necessary for learning and growth. We become so entangled with the possibility of failure that we choose to play a much smaller game than we are capable of playing; we stick to things that are safe and easy.

The opposite side of playing it safe is taking enormous, impetuous risks. (Who cares? I'm going to fail anyway.) Taking risks is no longer a tool for growth and learning; it manifests itself as taking foolish chances. The result is the same: failure.

### 5. Fear of Poverty.

Over 21% of children in the United States alone are raised in poverty, and our imaginings cannot even come close to the poverty in some Third World countries. We know what real poverty is, but it doesn't have half the power as imagined poverty.

Buried underneath the fear of poverty is the dreaded specter of death. Our survival is threatened when we imagine not having enough to eat or a safe place to sleep. It touches our most primitive concerns. But the fear of not having enough can be as destructive as the reality.

We create our own brand of poverty. We may choose to spend more than we make; we then try to earn more, but we spend more than we have again. Or we put everything we earn under the mattress, in the bank, or between the pages of a book. Our car may be falling apart or our clothes in shreds, but we choose, out of the fear of not having enough, to save the money we earn rather than spend it. The prophecy is self-fulfilled; we feel poor.

### 6. Fear of Commitment.

Commitment can represent loss of control and freedom. It is an act of vulnerability and courage. We may fear that once we make a commitment, we can't go back; but no one—no parent, teacher, government official or manager—can make you commit to anything if you don't want to. You may say yes, you may go through the motions, but you will be operating out of compliance, not commitment. You will only truly commit when, for you, the payoff is greater than the sacrifice.

Fear is an incredibly strong emotion, but it usually triggers a negative response. How can we turn that powerful emotion into something that can work for us? This requires a major shift in thinking.

Recall something from your past that scared you, or think of something awful that could happen in the future. Write it down and think about it long and hard.

_____

Pay attention to your body. Where do you feel the fear? Do you feel discomfort in your stomach, chest, shoulders, or does it make your hands sweat?

_____

You may tell yourself you're not afraid, but your body will always know what's going on. The messages you receive by paying attention to your body will be signals that something is wrong, needs to be prevented, or needs to be changed.

Now think of something which excites you. When was a time you remember being excited?

_____

How did your body react? Write in detail how you react to excitement.

_____

_____

Review what you wrote. Do you see any similarities?

_____

_____

_____

You can turn fear into power by simply changing your point of view.

Recall the paradoxical cube. You could determine which side of the cube was prominent by simply deciding which one you wanted to stand out. Nothing changed except how you looked at the cube. You can turn fear into power the same way.

Conscious shifts in the way you see things can take place when you challenge what you believe to be true. You can do that when you see and recognize the illusions that create fear where there could be power.

## THE THREE GREAT ILLUSIONS

### 1. The Illusion of Separability

This is the belief that you are totally separate from the rest of the world, that your actions do not directly impact others. At home, you believe that your behavior has no effect on your family. At work, you think your performance does not influence the success of the corporation.

The Illusion of Separability is supported by the family unit, our educational system and the organizational structure where the reward system focuses on individual efforts rather than the family, team, community or organization. It can be frightening to think that every time you make a phone call, smile, frown, get angry, discipline, blame, love, act or not act, that you directly affect people. The awareness of your personal power to affect others can be an awesome sense of responsibility and accountability.

Whether you like it or not, you have a tremendous amount of influence on those around you. And those people you have influenced continue to spread your influence like a circle of ripples in a pond. Influence creating influence: cause and effect. Once you shift your thinking, you experience a connection with others. You will also discover one of your most important assets for creating a successful life: the people around you.

### 2. The Illusion of Failure

Of the six major fears (rejection, success, failure, commitment, poverty, change), failure is the one that always puts the brakes on creativity, growth and productivity. Most of us have been programmed to fear failure, but it is the individual who looks at failure in a positive way who is able to take the Quantum Leap. Feedback from our failures gives us the necessary information to do a course correction.

Failure is a by-product of creativity, learning, and risk-taking, those things which make life exciting, passionate and fun. There is no growth without risk-taking, and there is no possibility of risk-taking without failure.

Think of three events in your life which you or someone else labeled as failure and ask yourself what you learned from them. Sometimes we learn from our own mistakes, and sometimes we learn from the mistakes of others.

### 3. The Illusion of Consciousness

It is a natural assumption that the choices we make are simple acts of will. We go through life making choices, reacting to external forces and exerting our will when we can. This is the Illusion of Consciousness.

When a hypnotist hypnotizes his subject, he guides that person into a state where conscious judgment is set aside and a suggestion can be momentarily or permanently programmed into the subconscious. These suggestions actually become the subject's reality, his or her personal paradigm, and he or she acts as though that suggestion were true.

Our socialization, what we've been taught, is like the hypnotist's programming, and our behavior is the result of those suggestions. Your programming contains not only positive, empowering beliefs, but also erroneous and negative junk programming. It doesn't matter: these are your core beliefs. They are usually unconscious and unexamined; yet every action you take and every decision you make is influenced by them.

Your willingness to examine your beliefs gives you the power to change them, and thereby change your reality: change failure into opportunity, change yourself from victim to creator, turn fear into power.

## TOOLS TO TURN FEAR INTO POWER

### 1) Define your behavior patterns.

Notice what you do when you're afraid and what situations trigger that behavior.

### 2) Record events.

Choose one incident representative of what you do when you're afraid. What frightened you and what did you do?

_____

Take the event apart as you would a clock, and you will began to notice how you tick. Recognition often allows you to discard self-sabotaging choices before the pattern is repeated.

### 3) Trace your fear to its source.
When was the last time this happened? The time before? Understanding plus forgiveness can provide the necessary energy to break self-sabotaging patterns.

### 4) Perform a reality check.
Is your fear is getting in the way of something you want? List three things that are being negatively affected by your fears.

1. _____

2. _____

3. _____

Choose the most important one and put an X next to it. Now re-evaluate that goal. Consider the sacrifices and payoffs if you were to commit yourself to achieving that goal.

What's the worst that can happen?      And the best?

_____      _____

_____      _____

_____      _____

_____      _____

Does the positive outweigh the negative? You turn fear into power when you are clear about what is real and what is imagined. Are your fears real?

If you feel you have chosen the correct direction, keep in mind your previous patterns of choice and the resulting behavior.

### 5) Tell people.

You gain power by sharing your fear with others. It takes courage to expose yourself, but the payoff is support and reinforcement of positive behavior.

### 6) Experience the fear and go ahead anyway.

Keep your goal firmly in mind. Recognize and accept that with every choice you make, you give up something and you gain something. Focus on what you gain and let go of the loss. Do not give up, keep your word to yourself, and do what you have to.

The illusions of Separability, Failure, and Consciousness are the three giant stumbling blocks to changing fear into power. As you explore your belief systems and focus on your priorities, you will see options which were previously invisible. When you explore the possibility of being connected to others instead of being separate, transform failure into feedback and learning, turn judgment into curiosity and become aware of the strength of the subconscious, you have acquired power. I think the choice to ignore the power of fear is the most frightening prospect of all.

# QUANTUM LEAP THINKPOINTS

Fear does not actually exist.

Fear is False Evidence Appearing Real.

As long as you continue to grow,
fear will always be your partner.

You create your own brand of poverty through fear.

You lessen the power of fear
by acknowledging it, both to yourself and others.

You can change failure into opportunity by learning.

To ignore the power of fear
is the most frightening prospect of all.

# YOUR TURN

There are six basic fears—**Rejection, Change, Success, Failure, Poverty** and **Commitment**—all of which stem from an elemental fear of loss. You experience a level of all these fears whether or not you admit to it.

**Consider** how these fears work themselves into your life by acknowledging **what you might lose** ...

1. ... if you are REJECTED:

_____

_____

2. ... if things CHANGE: (like your job or your relationship)

_____

_____

3. ... if you become a SUCCESS:

_____

_____

4. ... if you FAIL:

_____

_____

5. ... if you lived in POVERTY:

_____

_____

6. ... if you made a COMMITMENT

_____

_____

Read over your own remarks and PAY ATTENTION to your body's reaction. What are you really afraid of?

Can you turn that into power?

## Point #3

# *HOLD A VISION*

**T**ake a rubber band and stretch it between your hands. What does the stretching produce? Tension. If you release one end of the rubber band, it will snap toward the secured end, and the tension disappears.

Imagine tying one end of a mental rubber band around your entire being and the other end around what you imagine is your ideal future. If this vision of your future is solidly in place, and you let go of the world around you, you will be propelled toward that future. You whisk past barriers, problems, and all other negative circumstances until the tension is satisfied. This energy to move forward is exactly what a vision provides.

A vision is like a lighthouse: it illuminates rather than limits, gives direction rather destination. All successful individuals and organizations have this in common: a positive, meaningful vision of the future supported by a series of compelling goals.

What exactly *is* a vision? It may be eliminating world hunger, cleaning up the environment, or improving the lives of the people around us; but a vision is always greater than ourselves. Vision expresses our deepest values about work, family, achievement or community. Vision transforms momentary strategies into a way of life. Vision engenders change. It plays a core role in our choice of career, our mates, where we live and what we do.

It is a common misunderstanding to equate a personal goal with a vision. But the differences are vast. A goal comes from the head; a vision comes from the heart.

A goal is a baby step toward a vision. A goal may be short-term or long-term; it has a beginning and an end. But a vision is an on-going process. A goal is task-oriented; a vision is process-oriented. A goal is limiting; a vision is open-ended. A goal is often boring, mundane

and non-inspirational, but a vision provides energy, power and passion. A vision creates the energy to achieve the goals.

## THE ELEMENTS OF A VISION

### 1. VISION IS ABOUT OTHERS

Challenge the short-term, quick-result, "me, me, me" way of thinking. A vision of greatness must focus on adding value to and empowering others. A vision is about what we offer one another; it is an act of service. A vision inspires commitment because it is worth pursuing for its own sake.

### 2. VISION IS SPIRITUAL AND IDEALISTIC

Our day-to-day existence is cluttered with practical matters. We're busy and distracted and we have our own priorities. Things get done when we find the time and energy for them. However, when we appeal to the idealistic part of our nature, and touch the spirit, we tap into an enormous reserve of both time and energy.

Vision is more powerful than logic. It may be impractical or unreasonable or lofty. It requires us to stretch. It may appear to ask too much of us. If so, then you're on the right track.

### 3. A VISION IS AUTHENTIC

Authenticity means the vision comes from you. No one can make the statement for you. It must be personal in order to "own" it. The vision must be an extension of your personal being.

### 4. A VISION IS EXTRAORDINARY

A vision requires sacrifice, and we don't make sacrifices for the dull and ordinary. A vision must take a quantum leap from the mundane. If it spells out our highest ideals and wishes, it stands to reason that it will stand above the commonplace. It will be radical and outrageous. It will set us apart form the crowd.

### 5. A VISION IS VALUE-BASED.

Your personal values form the basis of and create the energy for your vision. Values act as a compass to guide our day-to-day decisions in the right direction.

You are going to create your own personal vision, keeping in mind the five elements. To help you do that, I designed several exercises in self-reflection.

Sometimes the easiest way to define your vision is to start at the end of your life and look backwards. Although somewhat uncomfortable, this exercise almost always touches the heart of what you want and need.

Place a dot at the point in the spiral where you imagine you are now

**Your Death**

**Your Birth**

and draw a horizontal line through it. Notice the length of time on either side on the line.

Now ask yourself some questions.

What contributions have you already made in your lifetime?

_____
_____
_____

What you would you like to contribute in the time remaining?

_____
_____
_____
_____

What do you want most from life?

_____
_____
_____

Write a sentence for your tombstone. It should represents the essence of who you are and what you want people to know about you.

Here lies _____
_____
_____
_____

Make a list of your own strengths and weaknesses. Don't let modesty or fear stand in the way of an honest list.

STRENGTHS                    WEAKNESSES

_____    _____
_____    _____
_____    _____
_____    _____
_____    _____
_____    _____

Now cover up the list of weaknesses. When you focus on your positive attributes, you solidify your own foundation and zero in on what makes you unique. Set your modesty aside. Acknowledge the goodness, wisdom and specialness of yourself. Celebrate who you are. Appreciate yourself.

And write it down.

I am...

_____

_____

_____

Complete that sentence with whatever comes to your mind. Now do it again.

I am ...

_____

_____

_____

In fact, write as many "I AM ..." sentences as you can. Include your talents, characteristics, and personality traits. If you run out of personal viewpoints, invent some. You may be surprised at some of the insights you discover about yourself.

I AM ....

_____

_____

_____

_____

_____

_____

_____

_____

It's time to put your Grand Vision to paper. Re-write it as many times as you wish. It may take you an hour, a day, a week or even more for you to write it down, and it is never finished. Over the years, you may change, alter or add to it.

Remember the elements of a vision.

... about others.

... spiritual and idealistic.

... authentic.

... extraordinary.

... consistent with your values.

Vision is a whole much greater than its parts; it cannot be built by simply assembling its pieces. However, assembling its pieces is the only way to begin.

Write yours here:

## MY GRAND VISION

# QUANTUM LEAP THINKPOINTS

Vision is more powerful than goals.

A vision creates energy.

A vision comes from the heart.

Touch the spirit and you tap into enormous reserves.

Like a lighthouse, a vision provides illumination and direction.

Values act as a compass.

# YOUR TURN

You have just spent some time creating your own GRAND VISION. You wrote it down on Page 47.

**Consider** that you were too limiting; your schemes were too earthbound, too small, too logical, too practical.

**Expand** your vision. Think bigger. Let your imagination free, but ask yourself: Is my vision about others? Serve others? Is it spiritual? Passionate? Is it based on my solid core values and principles?

Point #4

# *ENLARGE GOALS*

**A**s children, we were told, with great authority, how close to the edge we could walk, how high in the trees we could climb. We were warned about how much to expect from Santa, from our friends, and from ourselves.

Unfortunately, many of these restrictions were based on fear. The intention was admirable, meant to guide and help us in our growth to adulthood, but the end result was a transmission of limitations, feelings of powerlessness and unworthiness. We weren't big enough to go with daddy, old enough to cross the street by ourselves, or good enough to get what we wanted from Santa.

When we grew up, we put all those limitations into operation: we don't earn enough to buy that house, we aren't good enough to get that promotion, we aren't thin enough to be attractive.

If we truly believe ourselves, we set our sights a little lower, our goals smaller. We create a series of short-term, achievable goals. This is disappointing because we are built to strive, stretch and perform. When not put to our fullest use, we function, but at minimum capacity. Unless we consciously set goals that stretch us, we lock on to whatever is convenient. We may trundle after someone else's goals or trudge through life accomplishing a series of maintenance goals, cleaning the house when it doesn't need cleaning, organizing and reorganizing closets, or tinkering with the car. The illusion of accomplishment and forward movement is created, but we are merely treading water. We can't see possibilities, because, for us, they do not exist. When we become dedicated to short-term goals, we cement our rudders in place, and we are unable to adjust our sails. In our personal lives, we become frustrated and unmotivated. At work, the goals become equated with boredom and deadlines, demands and overtime. We work without passion and without commitment. We limit ourselves without knowing it.

Goals and goal-setting are not the problem. Maintenance goals are necessary; they are a way of keeping score. But they do not make for a life driven by vision and supported by accomplishment. They contain their own built-in blinders.

The moment we set a goal, we put a ceiling on our possibilities. Remember, goals come from the head; vision comes from the heart. **Goals must be vision-driven**. Goals are created by and in turn support our personal vision.

Without clearly declared goals and a plan of action to achieve them, you will most likely spend your life wondering why others get what they want while you settle for mediocrity. But only you can ignite the energy necessary for leaping to a new level.

Write down a goal which you would like to achieve.

_____

Now what can you add to that goal? Make it bigger and brighter.

_____

And bigger and brighter still ...

_____

_____

Whenever you set a goal, you have the conscious choice to make it a stretch-goal by simply thinking bigger. Challenge your assumptions about what's possible, and make your goal bigger yet.

_____

_____

Visualization is the most powerful tool you have for attaining the goals you've set. Visualization mobilizes and focuses your own resources. By applying the techniques for effective visualization, you can reduce stress, improve your golf game or lose weight. And you already know how to do it.

## IT'S EASY.

Imagine yourself lying on the beach, waves gently lapping at the shore, breeze blowing the smell of salt air. Feel it.

Now imagine yourself skiing. Feel the icy chill against your skin and hear the crunch of the edges of your skis cutting powder.

Now think of a fire engine racing through the streets of your neighborhood, the sense of urgency and potential terror centered in your chest.

Visualize, picture, feel and sense. You can take yourself through a series of emotions and feelings that are almost real, simply by _thinking_. Imagine taking a bite out of a ripe and juicy lemon, and you can even produce an actual biochemical reaction in your body. Doesn't it make you wince and your mouth water?

That's how easy visualization is. Visualize your goals consistently, and you can make them real.

## TECHNIQUES FOR VISUALIZATION

1) **Be clear about what you want.**

Write a list of everything you want to achieve and want to do. Review the list several times and eliminate those goals that seem weak. Eliminate goals which you chose because they are expected of you by someone else.

2) **Align your goals with your values**.

Your goals must reflect what you value most in your life. Do the goals you visualize support your personal vision?

### 3) **Put yourself in a relaxed, receptive state**.

Relax. This quiets your mind-chatter and opens your subconscious to receive mental pictures.

The easiest method of relaxation is to recall a place where you have felt at peace - maybe a vacation you took or a childhood playground. Shut your eyes and use your imagination.

Or use a "point-by-point" relaxation. Find a quiet place, sit in a comfortable chair, dim the lights, and close your eyes. Take a moment to become aware of the temperature of the room, the pressure of your body against the chair, your breathing, and the beat of your heart.

Tense your body and then relax. Let the tension go, one portion of your body at a time, beginning with your face, moving to your shoulders, then your arms, hands, stomach, and legs. Tense each point fiercely and then relax.

Slowly inhale through your nose and exhale through your mouth, then move your concentration throughout your body again, focusing on relaxing specific areas. Concentrate and relax.

### 4) **Make your visualization real.**

Experience your desired outcome as if it were already happening. Make the visualization specific and detailed. See it, hear it, taste it, smell it and feel it.

### 5) **Energize your visualization.**

Give it as much high-powered emotion as you can. When you attach positive emotions and enthusiasm throughout your process of mental rehearsal, you add energy to the process.

### 6) **Visualize often**.

The more you visualize, the more power you give to your subconscious.

### 7) **Visualize before you go to sleep.**

If you choose to visualize once a day, do it just before you go to sleep. While your conscious mind sleeps, your subconscious is still on the job. The subconscious takes what it is given, categorizes, organizes, files and makes sense out of things. Feed the subconscious the material to work with just before you go to sleep, and you give it six to eight hours to work on your desired outcomes.

### 8) Support your visualization with affirmations.

Tell yourself, "I deserve this. I am becoming what I want to be." Write your affirmations on paper and carry them with you, hang pictures on the wall, or record a cassette tape and play it for yourself.

### 9) Trust and be patient.

Commit to your routine, focus on your outcome often, affirm, and then let go, trust and give the process time to work.

### 10) Be grateful.

When you achieve your goals, give thanks. You did a good job and deserve to acknowledge it.

Here's a wonderful story about limiting goals.

A young man is learning the strategy of visualization. He imagines driving a Corvette. He pictures himself behind the wheel. He feels the power as he accelerates. He hangs a picture of a Corvette above his desk and carries another in his wallet.

A close friend, knowledgeable about visualization, but also about stretch-goal thinking, sees how his friend is approaching his process. Pulling his friend aside, he says, "You're thinking pretty small, aren't you?"

Our young man is stunned. "What do you mean? I'm visualizing my goal in great detail and supporting it with visual reminders. What else can I do?"

"Let me ask you a question," says his friend. "Do you have a relationship that's important to you?"

"No," our young man replies. "But I hope to."

"Well," responds the friend, "why don't you visualize the perfect woman sitting beside you in your Corvette?"

"That's a great idea!" So our young man creates a mental picture that includes the ideal woman.

Time goes by, and the friend asks our young man how his mental exercise was going.

"Great," says the young man. "I feel myself driving my car and I see the woman with all the qualities I desire sitting next to me."

His friend, relentless in the pursuit of excellence, tells him, "You're still think pretty small, aren't you?"

"What are you talking about? I'm visualizing the perfect woman sitting beside me in the perfect car. What more can I have?"

"A lot," his friend advises wisely. "Why don't you visualize the perfect woman sitting beside you in the perfect car parked in front of your ideal house?"

"Oh, come on," our man counters. "You know I can't afford the house."

## YOU AND YOUR RAS

You have a screening device in your brain called the **R**eticular **A**ctivating **S**ystem or RAS. Basically, your RAS determines what you pay attention to. Your conscious mind can only pay attention to a limited amount of the stimuli with which you are constantly bombarded. To keep your sanity, you must filter out the majority of the incoming information. Your RAS determines what's important and what's superficial, it allows you to focus on what you *believe* is important. For example, you will remember from this workbook only the information which you believe is pertinent to you; your RAS will screen out the rest.

Your RAS is neither good nor bad; it simply allows the information in which supports what you believe. In short, you see what you believe. If you could train your mind to notice that which supports your goals, you would be attracted to the resources necessary. And if you could train your mind to break the limitations of your own goal-setting, you could be capable of incredible things.

Let's forget about goals for the moment and think about dreams. Dreams are your private, personal, secret wish-list. There are no boundaries or restrictions to dreaming. Dreams spark the creative spirit, and the beauty of dreams is they are endless. List 50 dreams. Be crazy, irrational, and impractical. List hopes, fantasies, and desires. On this page, they are all yours. You have no limits.

Turn for your dream page...

List your dreams:

If you are like most people, you had some doubts as you wrote. Some of your ideas may be impractical and downright foolish. Great. You stirred up your imagination. You can get practical later.

Congratulations! You have just done what most of us never dare to do. You have acknowledged your dreams. This is the first step to making them come true. Dreams are nothing more than goals in the making.

# QUANTUM LEAP THINKPOINTS

We are built to strive, stretch and perform.

The moment we set a goal, we set a limit on our possibilities.

Goals must be vision-driven.

Visualization is the tool with which you create your reality.

Many of our limitations are based on fear.

1. Visualize
2. Take action
3. Reinforce your visualization

Dreams are only goals in the making.

# YOUR TURN

Let's **forget** about dreams for the moment and **think** about goals. You probably have some very real ones that you are working on right this moment.

Visualize them complete. Visualize them already done. Separately, one-by-one. Write them down as if you have already achieved them.

1._____

2._____

3._____

How does that make you feel? If you **vividly** imagined your goals achieved, you will feel energized and committed to making it happen. That feeling of power and commitment is fuel for success.

You can come back to this page once every day, close your eyes, and bring that feeling back. When you do, think about making those goals a little bigger each time, and add small, enhancing details to each one.

# Point #5

# *BE FLEXIBLE*

**C**lasp your hands together as demonstrated in the diagram below:

Now take your hands apart and clasp them back together moving your fingers over one digit. What words would you use to describe the difference between the two? Strange, weird, unbalanced, different, uncomfortable, odd, silly, awkward? Wrong?

All these words describe how we unconsciously respond to change, yet with a slight shift of perspective, that change in your handclasp might be considered new, interesting, curious, or pleasant.

Now make a fist with either one of your hands and press the fist against the palm of your opposite hand. Press harder. Did you resist by pressing back against your fist with the palm of your opposite hand? Chances are, you did. Resistance is a natural part of the human spirit.

There is constant, unrelenting change in nearly every area of our lives, and we resist unconsciously. We resist changes in technology, new products, new services, new marketing and new selling techniques. At work, we watch with dismay as barriers between departments crumble and partnerships form between competitors. In our schools, slow learners and kids in wheelchairs are integrated into regular classrooms. Administrators, teachers, parents and the community are coping with new math, interactive reading machines, and schools without walls. The American family has been remolded. Single-parent families outnumber dual-parent homes, and same-sex partners are raising children. Children from divorced parents grow up in every-other-weekend situations.

Change is unsettling; it's scary. We don't care if it's change for the better; most of us resist it. We like the status quo. There is a strange comfort in thinking we can anticipate our future, even if the future is black. We may stay in an unrewarding job because the thought of changing jobs is makes us feel insecure. We may resist a regular exercise program because we don't know how people will react to us if our looks change. Even battered wives have admitted that an abusive marriage is easier to accept than the prospect of divorce.

Yet how would you feel if you knew with absolute certainty that every day would be exactly like the day before? You would probably do everything in your power to shake things up. We resist and crave change, a paradox that creates unconscious, involuntary behavior that is usually counter-productive and often destructive. But this much is sure: there is nothing so constant as change.

Have you ever cried at a sad movie? That's because the subconscious cannot tell the difference between a real or an imagined experience. Natural resistance to change is similar in that our defenses cannot distinguish between change for the better or change for the worse. We resist **all** change—for three big reasons:

1. **The threat of loss.**

   All change involves giving up something. We feel victimized, vulnerable, helpless and powerless, which makes us hurt and angry, sometimes even physically ill. Unless we learn to develop flexibility, we can only see the loss, and loss is painful.

2. **Homeostasis.**

   It's tough enough to have the threat of loss challenge us, but we also have a personal built-in mechanism, like the thermostat in a home, that we must learn to deal with. Our body temperature and blood sugar levels are two examples of this safety valve, but our personal thermostat goes beyond our bodies. We buffer ourselves against the shock of change by acting in familiar ways with familiar habits and behavior from the past. It's involuntary. Like the home thermostat, we're pre-programmed.

This condition of equilibrium is called homeostasis, a universal stamp of all self-regulatory systems from the bacterium to the salamander, from the human being to the family, from an organization to a culture.

Homeostasis applies to everything. A golfer says to himself after a particularly terrific round of golf, "I can't believe how well I played today. It wasn't like me at all." The next day he plays one of the worst games of his life. He balanced himself out. Homeostasis was maintained; his personal thermostat was working.

### 3. The identification paradigm.

People who want to break long-time habits, like over-eating or smoking, have more to combat than homeostasis. They may drop a few pounds or go a few weeks without smoking, but in time, most people drift back to their old habits.

It's discouraging and frustrating, but understand that they probably encountered resistance from their families, friends and co-workers when they changed their everyday habits. We tend to be identified with our way of life. We may have inherited it or built it ourselves, but we tend to devote our creative energies to maintaining it.

Existing, familiar structures create an artificial comfort zone of convictions, routine, habits and rituals. If any of these infra-structures are challenged, the structure of the unit is challenged, and there's an unconscious, protective instinct which resists the change, no matter how beneficial. Identification can help keep intact the nurturing aspects of family, religion and even business, but for the most part, identification limits innovation, exploration and curiosity. A company exclusively identified with a specific type of product may not anticipate a need for a new product; a man who identifies only with a certain aspect of his career may not see the possibilities for advancement.

Add this to the natural tendencies of the internal thermostat and you have a tough combination to beat.

Flexibility is more than a willingness to change to suit conditions, more than reacting to crisis change and evolutionary change. Flexibility is creativity. If we are ever to <u>create</u> change, we must be willing to set aside our ego and judgment. We must be flexible enough to bend our most rigid beliefs. We need to notice, extract and make use of the opportunities at hand. Flexibility requires paying attention, so that we can select from what has existed in the past or exists in the present to form something new.

Think of a time when you were told you were being rigid, or a situation in which you considered yourself inflexible.

_____

_____

What were the negative results of your inflexibility?

_____

_____

_____

Examine your behavior at work or at home, as an employee, a manager, a partner or a parent. Are there areas where you could be more flexible?

_____

_____

_____

Is there a change you are involved in or that you are witnessing that troubles you?

_____

_____

If you were to set aside your need to be right, the comfort of the way things have always been, and the ease of the familiar, how could you mold or restructure that change to suit you?

_____

_____

_____

Is the effort worth it?

YES                              NO

That's what it's all about.

There may not be much you can do about what's changing in your personal life, your school, your organization, or in your community, but there is a lot you can do about how you react to it. Adapting to change is difficult to execute and painful in the process, yet much less exhausting than fighting it.

# QUANTUM LEAP THINKPOINTS

Resistance is a natural part of the human spirit.

The subconscious cannot tell the difference
between what is real and what is imagined.

All change involves giving up something.

We resist all change, no matter how beneficial.

Flexibility enhances creativity.

Adapting to change is less exhausting than fighting it.

# YOUR TURN

Make a decision that you will not say the words NO, CAN'T or IMPOSSIBLE today. Play the game of possibility. For one day, everything is possible.

You will need to create a mindset where that can happen. That means you will **have** to make everything work. Consider every solution. Pretend that every alternative is a viable one. You will have to be FLEXIBLE.

| | |
|---|---|
| You DO have the time to work out today. | Serve the family dinner one hour later today. |
| You CAN finish that report on time. | Go in the office one hour earlier and have lunch at your desk. |
| Your son CAN have an extra $10 this week. | Ask him to do the laundry or the breakfast dishes for you. |
| You WILL see that awful movie your wife wants to see. | You can see your movie another day. |

Commit to saying yes. Commit to making things happen instead of resisting, and take the time at the end of the day to write at least three examples of your flexibility instead of resistance.

What you wanted to resist:        How you made it work:

1. _____

_____

2. _____

_____

3. _____

_____

Are you happy? Remember, you can't say no.

Point #6

# *HAVE COMMITMENT*

Until one is committed, there is hesitancy,
the chance to draw back, always ineffectiveness.
Concerning all acts of initiative and creation,
there is one elementary truth, the ignorance of which
kills countless ideas and splendid plans:

> The moment one definitely commits oneself,
> then Providence moves, too. All sorts of
> things occur to help one that would never otherwise have
> occurred.

> A whole stream of events issues from the
> decision, raising in one's favor all manner
> of unforeseen incidents and meetings and material
> assistance, which no person could have dreamed
> would have come his way.

*—W.H. Murray*

Before I decided to buy a Land Cruiser, I never really noticed any on the road. However, the morning following my commitment to buy one, I went out for breakfast and I could swear the world had just given birth to Land Cruisers. They were everywhere. Obviously, they were always there, but I hadn't noticed them. If it works for Land Cruisers, why can't it work for anything within the power of our imagination? That's the magic: it can.

Commitment triggers a sort of inner visualization. It provides you with an unconscious awareness. When you make a commitment, you see things which had previously been invisible to you, possibilities your RAS had been filtering out. Commitment truly makes the invisible visible.

Top management consultant Ken Blanchard states, "There is a great difference between simple interest and commitment. When you are interested in doing something, you do it only when it's convenient. When you are committed to something, you accept no excuses, only results."

Commitment gives strength, energy and direction. It creates seemingly magical outcomes. You may wish to look at the phenomenon as extracting from the universe what we need to support our commitment. Whatever view you choose to take, the end result is the same. It works like magic. People who are committed are passionate and enthusiastic. They have power and resources. They have developed courage and the willingness to take risks. We know all that, and yet the fear of commitment is one of our most basic fears. If you can imagine total commitment without thinking about what you might lose or jeopardize, you are among the very few.

We wish and fantasize and may even have good intentions, but without commitment, we change our minds, we are bored, and we fill our lives with complaints. We find excuses, drag ourselves out of bed to go to work, and concern ourselves with simple survival. Too many of us view ourselves as victims with no control of our destiny.

Commitment is taking a stand, regardless of circumstances or what people say or do to discourage you. It is keeping your word at all costs. The choice of personal commitment is vast: commitment to your family, your career, your health, your personal or organizational vision or service to others.

What is <u>your</u> definition of the word "commitment"?

_____

What things come to mind when you think about commitment, yours or anyone else's?

_____

_____

_____

Now think of three areas where you would <u>like</u> to commit yourself—a relationship, for example, or a passion like painting or music.

1._____

2._____

3._____

Have you encountered resistance? You must have, or you would have made the commitment already. Where do you encounter the most resistance?

_____

_____

Are YOU on that list?

**Commit** comes from the Latin "committere," which means to ignite action: "to bring together, join, entrust, and **do**." Commitment emerges from the decision to <u>do</u> something. It blossoms from our own desires. It is a promise of the heart from which you will move forward, no matter the resistance.

70

## COMMITMENT = DETERMINATION = ACTION

All of us are quite capable of superior performance and we can create a great amount of self-motivation by committing to something greater than ourselves. Positive pressure can also be self-induced when we commit to personal excellence or when we want to please a coach, a boss or a loved one.

Developing commitment is a skill you can learn. Start easy. Choose one <u>very</u> simple and easy short-term goal or activity to which you think you can commit yourself for one week only. Just one week. Anything from taking a 10-minute walk every morning to writing in your journal, spending 5 minutes with your son or daughter to a half-hour reading a book.

_____

_____

_____

What excuses do you make for NOT doing that activity? What is your resistance?

_____

_____

Understand the resistance and do it anyway. For one week. Make a commitment.

I, _____, promise to
                    *(Your name here)*

_____  _____
         *(Your commitment here)*
every day for **one full week**, starting now.

_____
        *(Sign here)*

After the week is over, choose a larger goal and do it again. Do it even if you are afraid to. Fear does not always translate into increased performance, but commitment does.


**Whatever you can do or dream you can do, begin it.**
**Boldness has genius and power and magic in it.**
**Begin it now.**

*—Goethe*

# QUANTUM LEAP THINKPOINTS

Commitment makes the invisible visible.

Commitment is a promise of the heart.

When you are committed, you accept no excuses.

You can create self-motivation when you commit to something greater than yourself.

Commitment always translates into increased performance.

# YOUR TURN

Go back to page 70, on which you listed three areas where you would like to commit yourself. Choose one of them.

I already asked you to think about what resistance you've encountered, but let's think positively here.

On the remainder of this page, write what you would do if you really were committed in that area of your life. Would you get up earlier? Practice more? Work harder? Move to a different city? Change jobs? Make a list.

And when you're done, mark one of them with an X.

And do it.

That's a start.

If I were truly committed, I would ....

## Point #7

# *EMPOWER*

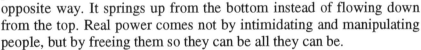

**W**hen you think of power, what images come to mind?

Often the word is associated with control. Those who have power are on top and in control. Switch the paradigm and you will see that real power works just the opposite way. It springs up from the bottom instead of flowing down from the top. Real power comes not by intimidating and manipulating people, but by freeing them so they can be all they can be.

Does managing with an iron hand get results? Of course it does. If employees are managed by heavy-handed bureaucratic control, employees will do their jobs. If children are threatened, they often do what they're told. But results will be short-term. Commitment and morale will be low; there will always be subtle rebellion. The iron hand creates a fear-based environment; fear stifles risk-taking and creativity. You may get what you asked for, but you can be sure you won't get anything more. People will comply, but they won't commit.

In the workplace, lightning-fast changes in technology and the marketplace, increased consumer awareness, and the communication explosion make it impossible for those sitting at the top of the organization to receive information quickly enough. Employees who are closer to the customer and their co-workers are key to keeping a competitive edge. Employees must have the authority to make rapid decisions without the fear of being punished. Empowerment is not an option here, **but a necessity**.

On a personal level, understand that most people realize a small fraction of their full potential simply because they don't feel a sense of power. Bureaucratic management or dominating parents do little to encourage initiative and peak performance. If the power rests at the top, underlings feel powerless, become unmotivated, and settle for mediocrity. The secret to successful management, parenting, and partnering lies in learning how to release the hidden potential of others.

## 10 PRINCIPLES FOR EMPOWERMENT

### 1. ASK FOR HELP

The mere act of asking for help sends a message to others that you value them and respect their opinions.

### 2. GIVE AUTHORITY ALONG WITH RESPONSIBILITY

You have to let go of the thought that you can do it better and faster. You must give authority equal to the responsibilities assigned. People need the necessary authority to carry out the tasks.

### 3. EXPECT EXCELLENCE

Set standards that stretch people beyond their self-imposed

limits. Expect resistance, but it's only when people are stretched that they discover talents they never knew they had and tap into their hidden personal power.

## 4. PROVIDE TRAINING

Provide the training necessary for people to live up to those standards. You wouldn't ask a man to be your chauffeur if he didn't know how to drive. Provide people with the necessary skills to accomplish their jobs. You want to give people every chance possible to meet with success. Training builds confidence and self-esteem.

## 5. SHARE INFORMATION

Never withhold information. Empowerment means providing the knowledge to make the necessary decisions to meet performance standards. Managers gain power when their employees are well- informed. Parents encounter less resistance from their children when children know why and how.

## 6. LISTEN AND RESPOND WITH EMPATHY

People want to be heard. Listening is healing. Let go of the need to justify or defend and walk in the other person's shoes. Create a space where people can express their fears without being made wrong. You empower by letting others know they are of value simply by listening.

## 7. PROVIDE CONSISTENT FEEDBACK

If people are to move to new heights of excellence, they must know how they are performing and what they need to improve. We often fail to give proper feedback because we assume people know when they are doing a good job. The eye cannot behold itself. People can't evaluate their own performance. Often we are too busy to stop and look inward.

Give feedback as close to the completion of the task as possible. Feedback not only reinforces positive performance but also shows a person how and when he needs to improve. Feedback builds pride, enhances self-esteem and motivates.

## 8. GIVE PEOPLE PERMISSION TO FAIL

When people are afraid to fail, they play it safe. No mistakes, but no growth. Their reach never exceeds their grasp. Goals are set low. Mediocrity is a comfortable way of life.

By giving people permission to fail, you empower them to take risks, stretch and move beyond their limits. You free their most powerful tool, their imagination.

Create an environment where people are not afraid to fail. Become a coach, not a cop.

### 9. TREAT PEOPLE WITH DIGNITY AND RESPECT

To know the truth of this, all you will have to do is ask yourself how you feel when you are treated with disrespect.

### 10. RECOGNIZE AND REWARD ACHIEVEMENT

When people feel like winners, they act like winners. There is no mystery here.

Test yourself on your empowerment skill, and list below specific action steps you can take in the empowerment process:

When do you have the opportunity to ask for help in solving a problem?

_____

_____

To whom can you give more authority to carry out their designated responsibilities?

_____

_____

What new stretch-goals can you set for yourself, your family members or employees?

_____

_____

What additional training and support can you provide?

_____

_____

What new information do you need to share?

_____

_____

With whom can you spend more time listening?

_____

_____

What systems can you put into effect which will allow others to express their fears or concerns without judgment?

_____

_____

How can you increase your flow of feedback? Consider small gestures like a smile or a thank-you as well as the obvious places for feedback, like staff meetings and counseling.

_____

_____

Have you ever punished failure? What specific actions can you take to set up an environment where people can take risks and are not afraid to fail?

_____

_____

What do you need to change about your attitude, behavior or actions to clearly demonstrate that you respect the dignity of the individual?

_____

_____

What specific actions can you take to reward and recognize others for their achievements and contributions? (i.e. genuine praise, monetary reward, increased authority, promotions, gifts, flowers?)

_____

_____

What specific people do you need to reward and recognize?

_____

_____

_____

Power operates under the same principle as love. The more you give to others, the more you receive in return.

**By giving up power, you gain more power.**

This is a paradox you must become comfortable with. If you want to achieve ultimate power for yourself, you must get out of your own way. Instead of depleting your energy trying to amass as much power as you can for yourself, focus your energy on empowering your friends, family or employees. You will be surprised at how high you will be lifted on their shoulders.

# QUANTUM LEAP THINKPOINTS

Training builds confidence and self-esteem.

Training comes before empowerment.

Real power works from the bottom up.

Fear stifles risk-taking and creativity.

You gain power by giving up power.

Control never creates long-term commitment.

The secret to success is releasing the potential of others.

# YOUR TURN

Choose four tasks you could delegate to someone else.

1. _____

2. _____

3. _____

4. _____

More important than choosing the person to whom you can delegate is examining why you haven't delegated those tasks already.
Why are you holding on to the tasks?

1. _____

2. _____

3. _____

4. _____

Now write what good will come of delegating those chores. Focus on yourself first and then on those around you, including the person to whom you are delegating.

Think of delegating as EMPOWERING. You haven't just given someone something to do; you have trusted someone, respected someone, complimented someone. What are the positive results of this empowerment?

1. _____

2. _____

3. _____

4. _____

Point #8

# COMMUNICATE WITH INTEGRITY

**in-te-gri-ty** (in teg´ri tê) *n.* 1. soundness of moral principles and character; uprightness; honesty. 2. state of being whole or undiminished, a wholeness or an unimpaired condition.

**W**hen architects and builders refer to a building's structural integrity, they are using the second definition, but I feel the same concept can be applied to human beings. The greater our integrity (using the first definition), the greater our completeness and wholeness. Communicating with integrity means expressing yourself in accordance with your moral principles, your values. Communication includes your actions, because what you do says more about what you believe than what you say. You are your word.

Values are our most personal, private and uniquely individual beliefs about what is important. They are the mental maps of the way we think things should be. They are our deepest convictions, and when we betray them, we destroy the integrity of our personal architecture.

Take a holistic approach and regard your life as a system. When all the areas of your life are in balance, you resonate; you are in tune with yourself. Harmony is the closest word I can find to describe it, and when you are in harmony, Quantum Leaps take place naturally.

But how can we know when we have spoken or acted against what's most important to us if we don't know what that is? Understanding your own value system will help you communicate more honestly. Understanding your value system will help you resonate.

Review this suggested list of values. There can be more or less, but this is a good place to start. See if you can choose six that you feel are important to you.

| | | |
|---|---|---|
| Honesty | Love | Freedom |
| Compassion | Trust | Family |
| Service to others | Self-growth | Reputation |
| Emotional health | Humility | Self-Respect |
| Money | Power | Sex |
| Physical health | Pleasure | Adventure |
| Peace of mind | Spirituality | Fame |
| Happiness | Creativity | Companionship |
| Wisdom | Excitement | Success |
| Challenge | Accountability | Perseverance |
| Diligence | Discipline | Thrift |
| Intimacy | Kindness | Acceptance |
| Fairness | Courage | Flexibility |
| Honor | Security | Recognition |
| Career | Leadership | Openness |
| Patience | Forgiveness | Comfort |
| Passion | Cheerfulness | Intelligence |
| Accomplishment | Gratefulness | |

Write the six values you have chosen here:

_____    _____

_____    _____

_____    _____

There is <u>always</u> one value which is most important, one core value which drives all the choices you make. In order to determine which one that is, you'll need to go through a unique questioning process. For the purpose of example, I'll use the six values I chose as my own:

Love          Freedom
Contribution    Honesty
Loyalty        Integrity

Is love more important than contribution? Love and contribution are closely linked, but you must choose one. I decide that love is more important than contribution, and I now use love as my primary comparison value to challenge the other values.

Is love more important than freedom? I have, in my past, assumed freedom was my most important value and made disastrous decisions based on that. At the time I was convinced that freedom was more important than anything, but now I see that I was wrong: when I really think about it, love is more important to me than freedom.

Is love more important than honesty? Yes. Is love more important than integrity? Yes. Is love more important than loyalty? This was the most difficult of all. I am fiercely loyal to my friends and I feel love and loyalty are closely linked. But I must eliminate one of the two values. The answer is yes. Love is more important than loyalty. So love is my number one core value. Now I need to choose my second most important value.

Is freedom more important than loyalty? No. I can cross that one out and switch, using loyalty as my comparison value. Is loyalty more important than contribution? Yes. Is loyalty more important than honesty? Yes. Integrity? Yes. I now know that loyalty is my number two core value.

I go through the same questioning process using each value as a comparison value and fix a priority to all six. Go back to your list and do the same for yourself.

I had been operating under the misconception that freedom was what I valued most. I made a lot of life choices based on that. No wonder I felt so restless, dissatisfied and unfulfilled when I had attained certain goals. You may surprise yourself as well. When you've finished your evaluation, write your core values in order of their importance:

1. _____

2. _____

3. _____

Are your words and actions reflecting these values, or have you communicated something else? Have you jeopardized the integrity of your personal architecture? When you do, the result can only be disaster.

Let's say Person **A**'s number one core value is freedom; Person **B**'s is family. They fall in love, marry and decide to have children. A makes a conscious decision to sacrifice freedom in order to raise a family, but of course says nothing. His (or her) actions say everything.

A feels trapped and takes the frustration out on the family. The children may grow up and leave home, but the damage has been done; and the miscommunication can be catastrophic for the couple's relationship. Had they each been aware of the other's values from the beginning, they could have talked about it and reached a possible compromise.

Let's go one step further. My father used to tell me, "Do as I say, not as I do." He said it with a smile, but that is the way many of us operate. Remember, you are your word. When you break your word, that's not what you do; it's who you are. It's only half the commitment to integrity when your words are true to your values. The other half is being true to your word. Keeping your word is mandatory to developing trust and communication. Whether you like it or not, you are a model. People are watching you. You are a leader. People are following you.

True magic happens when you take control of your value hierarchy. This may mean being conscious of your values, or it may mean placing a new value in your list. Some of us consciously choose to incorporate a core value such as playfulness, forgiveness, family, flexibility, courage or adventure and then choose daily actions which are congruent with the new core values.

Review your list. Are your values out of date? Are there new values which are more appropriate to your life and knowledge? Is there a value which would put your life more in balance?

If you have been acting consistently in a way which belies one or more of the values on your list, you are not in harmony and your list is probably in need of an overhaul. If you change your choice or order of values, give yourself a day or two and review your choices. Do a reality-check. If you're comfortable with your decision, commit to it and have the courage to view your life through your new value structure.

When you choose, commit, reinforce, and act consistently from your true values, you ring with harmony. The results are magical.

# QUANTUM LEAP THINKPOINTS

You are your word.

People become confused when
your actions are incongruent with your words.

Integrity is a personal state of wholeness.

People model your behavior.

One core value drives all the choices you make.

You are in control of your value hierarchy.

Integrity is harmony.

# YOUR TURN

Examine the three values you chose as your core values and review your actions and decisions over the past few months.

If there were times you acted against what you value, write the details here.

_____

_____

_____

_____

_____

_____

What were the results? Sometimes there is only an uncomfortable feeling when you compromise your integrity; other times, the results are extremely negative.

Now choose a decision you are facing now.

DECISION: _____

What are your alternatives and what are the values you may threaten?

| ALTERNATIVE | THREATENED VALUE |
|-------------|------------------|
| _____ | _____ |
| _____ | _____ |
| _____ | _____ |

Remember, when you act consistently with your values, you ring with harmony.

Point #9

# CREATE PARTNERSHIP

**W**e create partnerships for a variety of reasons, but the primary reason is for strength and resources. The bottom line is that we can <u>do</u> more when we have help.

We also create partnership for safety, for teamwork, and for love.

The need for a primary, loving relationship touches the very center of what it means to be human; it demands of us the courage to grow, stretch, learn and be vulnerable. It is only when we allow ourselves to be vulnerable that we become open to giving and receiving love and help honestly.

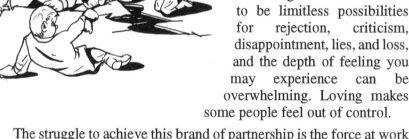

The willingness to be vulnerable is scary because we risk being hurt. There seems to be limitless possibilities for rejection, criticism, disappointment, lies, and loss, and the depth of feeling you may experience can be overwhelming. Loving makes some people feel out of control.

The struggle to achieve this brand of partnership is the force at work in novels and movies and poetry. It is at work all around you. Everyone wants to be partners with somebody, but how many successful partnerships do you see? Why is it so hard?

Ask yourself what a loving relationship looks like. How does it happen? What makes it work and how do you create one?

## 1) LOVE YOURSELF FIRST

It takes courage to make your own happiness your first priority in life, but when you do what feels right for you, you build personal integrity. Sometimes it will make others happy, and sometimes it won't.

Being true to yourself does not mean being self-centered or narcissistic. One of the greatest detriments to any relationship comes from expecting others to fill your void. The results are disastrous. There are enough hurdles to partnership without adding the strain of your neediness. When you nurture a loving relationship with yourself, you have built the foundation for creating other partnerships.

## 2) ACKNOWLEDGE YOUR FEARS

Partnerships tap into your most basic fears: loss of freedom and loss of control. They also open up opportunities for rejection, betrayal, entrapment, manipulation, and worst of all, unrequited love. If you associate fear with partnership, go through the following exercise.

1) Imagine what you are afraid of. What does it look like and feel like? Give the fear a shape, form, color and texture. Do you feel more than one fear? If so, see if you can discover the basic fear which supports the other fears.

2) Think positively about the fear. What does it have to teach you? Accept the possibility that you may have created the fear yourself. Did you create this fear to protect yourself from something?

3) How would you like your vision of an ideal partnership to look and feel? What images and emotions come to mind? What circumstances exist? What words would you use to describe an ideal partnership?

4) Move into and surround yourself with your ideal vision. Use your imagination. Open your heart. Create the vision as though it were a movie; then star in your movie.

5) Write down in detail your definition of an ideal partnership. If you become aware of any resistance, acknowledge it as fear, and keep writing.

### 3) ACCEPT PEOPLE AS THEY ARE

A partnership is a team, and the key to teamwork is synergy: the sum is greater than the parts. When two people form a commitment, a metaphorical third party is formed, which needs as much nurturing as does each of the parts separately.

Respect the needs of the individuals in your partnership. Take the time to discover their core values and make sure their values are honored and supported. As relationships change, so do needs. Be observant, ask questions and go out of your way to make sure your partners' values are fulfilled and you will experience the magic of a value-based relationship.

### 4) TELL THE TRUTH

It's easier to confide your deepest upsets and hurts to your barber than it is to the one we most need to communicate with, but without the courage to risk honest communication, there can be no quantum leaps.

Most of us don't want to make the people we work with or the people we love angry or disappointed. We're afraid to be rejected or betrayed or foolish. So we let the little things go. However, not communicating what may appear meaningless has what I call the Accumulation Effect. Pressure builds as the little frustrations and hurts accumulate until there is an explosion: anger, withdrawal, depression, betrayal. The irony is that whatever finally caused the explosion is almost never the real reason.

Reasons are stored up from the past, but the argument alone can permanently damage the partnership. All this frustration and attendant unhappiness could have been avoided had there been healthy communication.

Power struggles in a partnership are inevitable. Each person is a separate entity with separate beliefs, values and a point of view. Confrontations are an integral part of the dynamics of any meaningful, committed team. This is especially true as the paradigm shifts concerning the evolving roles of men and women in today's society. Points of view conflict.

The healthy solution to power struggles is communication, for all partners to express what they want and need and to confront the provocative situation immediately. Negotiation is the only solution.

Experience the fear and go for honest communication.

Don't blame. State what you feel. Don't suppress the little things.

### 5) RENEW PARTNERSHIPS

When a partnership is new, everyone spends a great deal of time communicating. We treat potential partners with respect, listening to their problems, and sharing our solutions. Then something peculiar begins to take place.

As relationships mature, we have a tendency to expect certain behavior. We criticize more; show appreciation less, anger more. We are less patient, and we spend less time listening. We forget what brought us together in the first place. The arrogance of assumption sets in. We believe our partners will be there forever, regardless of what we do or say.

Partnerships take work. Make it a daily practice to think of the goals which brought you together in the first place. Treat your partners as friends. Respect and value that friendship on a consistent basis. A garden has to be cultivated if you want it to grow. Cultivation of relationships is just as vital to keep any partnership alive and well.

Choose a partnership that is important to you. It could be your marriage, your relationship with your child or your boss, your best friend or your parents.

Now examine it through the filter of what you've read here. Does it pass the Quantum Test of Partnership?

YES   NO

1. Does your relationship allow you to honor your love for yourself?

2. Does this relationship allow you both to acknowledge your fears?

3. Do the two of you accept each other as you really are?

4. Do you tell each other the truth?

5. Have either you made efforts to keep the partnership fresh and renewed?

If your answer to that last one was NO, spend some time filling out the blanks below.

And then make sure you follow through.

## FOUR ACTION STEPS TO ENHANCE AN EXISTING PARTNERSHIP

1)_____

2)_____

3)_____

4)_____

# THE MAGIC OF TEAMS

Together
Everyone
Accomplishes
More

Teams present limitless possibilities for both short- and long-term partnerships. Teams have the potential to help us all solve problems and manage change smoothly, especially within an organizational structure like a school, government, or corporation. Teams can deal with overwhelming amounts of information, generate new ideas, and solve a multitude of problems. There is nothing new about teams. They have been around a long, long time.

Teams and teamwork are often used interchangeably. They work together, but they are not the same. A team is a small group of people with compatible and complementary skills committed to a common vision and specific, identifiable goals. Teamwork is a set of values: respect for the dignity of the individual, diversity, and superior communication. Large and complex organizations can never be a team. However, they can practice teamwork.

The formation and implementation of high performance or self-managed teams is not a quick-fix for deeply rooted organizational dysfunction. Teamwork takes time, patience, energy, commitment, knowledge, and tremendous resources, because it simply does not come naturally. The American culture is built on individualism. We praise individual achievement and excellence. Parents, teachers, coaches and role models in every area of life have helped convince us to look out for #1. We may use sports as a model for teamwork, but team sports are more about competition than teamwork. If they win, we lose.

There is often great resistance to participating in a team. We may not feel that we have the power to make decisions. We might not want to invest time and effort for someone else's benefit, or we don't want to work with a bunch of strangers. Basic human fears enter the picture: fear of talking in front of a group, fear of being punished for others' mistakes, or fear of confrontation.

However, we do have a handful of terrific examples of successful teams. Consider the movies THE MAGNIFICENT SEVEN, STAR TREK, STAR TREK: THE NEXT GENERATION, and VOYAGER. I always liked the Three Musketeers, too, but here is how I describe a successful team in my corporate presentations.

If you cut a photograph in half, what do you have? Two halves of a picture, totally separate and totally different—worth little unless they are pieced together. However, if you take a laser image, a hologram, and cut it in two pieces or a hundred pieces, every single piece would each contain the information of the whole. With one piece of a hologram, you can retrieve the information necessary to reconstruct the original, from a slightly different perspective.

Each piece of a hologram contains the information of the whole; each member of a team possesses the information of the whole team. Each team member is a part of the whole. You are me, and I am you. You cannot fail without me failing. You can't succeed without me succeeding. Competition can't exist. The Illusion of Separability is eliminated and we are personally accountable. We quit thinking "me" and start thinking "we."

The perfect model for the Holographic Team is making a movie. There is a strong vision (the script) which pulls everyone in the same direction. Several self-managed teams support the whole team, like wardrobe, set design, lighting, script development, and camera crews. There may be raging egos within each team, but the vision (script) is almost always strong enough to surmount challenges.

Forming teams for the sake of forming teams is a total waste of time and talent. In an organization, for example, management needs to see clearly that teams generate ideas and solutions to improve quality and productivity and that teams benefit the customer, shareholders and employees. There must be a clear and immediate business to drive the need for the team.

## Barriers to Creating Successful Teams

### 1. LACK OF VISION
The driving force must be a definable, realistic, and clearly communicated challenge with specific achievable objectives.

### 2. LACK OF COMMITMENT
People may do what they're told, but without commitment, they lack energy and force. Following instructions is merely compliance;

creativity and power come from commitment.

### 3. LACK OF TRAINING

Skills such as managing change, decision-making, conflict resolution, problem-solving, global thinking, and communication are as important as information. We cannot expect team members to get the job done without proper training.

### 4. CONTROL AND MANIPULATION

Teams must have freedom. The very nature of "team" demands that members be both trusted and empowered to fulfill their roles.

### 5. COMPETITION

Competition among team members, between team managers and members, or among teams within the same organization is destructive. The assumption that competition will increase performance is naive. Competition breeds information-hoarding and sabotage.

### 6. THE WRONG REWARD SYSTEM

Within a team, jobs and roles are often rotated which require members to learn new skills, and they expect to be compensated. Reward systems based on seniority won't work. You need to develop fair compensation for individual members as well as for the team itself.

Before you tackle the job of developing teams at work or school, or even at home, answer the following questions:

What do you believe is required to have an effective team?

1._____

2._____

3._____

4._____

What projects would lend themselves well to teams and teamwork?

1. _____
2. _____
3. _____
4. _____

What are some of your assumptions about yourself, your job, other people, or your organization that would influence successful teamwork?

1._____
2._____
3._____
4._____

What would have to change in order to build an effective team?

1._____
2._____
3._____
4._____

What specific beliefs, attitudes or fears do <u>you</u> have to change in order to become an effective team member?

1._____
2._____
3._____
4._____

What action steps can you take <u>NOW</u> to develop successful teams?

1._____

2._____

3._____

4._____

# QUANTUM LEAP THINKPOINTS

When you love and trust yourself,
you have a foundation for all partnerships.

Partnerships tap into basic fears.

Power struggles are inevitable.

Partnerships create synergy.

Teams succeed when driven
by a powerful, clearly communicated purpose.

Teams are every leader's greatest resource.

# YOUR TURN

You may not consider partnerships first when thinking about getting something done—whether it's personal or professional.

Maybe you should.

Pinpoint a task (challenge, chore, project, whatever) that you need to accomplish in the next few days or weeks.

_____

Who can help and how?

WHO                                        HOW

_____              _____
_____              _____
_____              _____

Why haven't you asked them to help you yet? What is your resistance? Remember that we can always get more done with the resources a partnership can offer. We can DO more when we have help.

## Point #10
# *HAVE FUN*

**O**f the 14 Points of Quantum Leap Thinking, this is easiest one to ignore and probably the last one most of us will commit to integrating into our daily lives. We have more important things to do, like making money and mending fences. Once we do all that, we'll get around to having fun. After all, we know life is hard.

You may think fun is a luxury, but that's not true; having fun is essential. Doctors will tell you that fun lowers blood pressure, increases energy, and helps fight infections. Therapists in hospitals schedule playtime for even the most seriously ill.

Fun is strong medicine because it affects those around us, too. Happiness invites conversation, friendship, interchange and support. It is attractive and infectious, capable of improving not only our general health and attitude, but our very chances for success.

Beyond the obvious lies a whole realm of life-enhancing opportunities. Fun promotes creativity and balances intellect with spirit. Fun renews, regenerates and satisfies. Without it, we feel resentful, tired, angry, put upon, overburdened, and victimized.

So why is our resistance to having fun so incredibly strong? Why is it the last thing on our list of priorities? Why, at the end of a long day, or at the end of the week, or, sadly, at the end of the year, do we realize that we haven't had any fun? That we put it off so long that it didn't get done at all?

Even though we know it's good for us, we think having fun is selfish. We haven't earned it. And if our self-esteem needs work, we don't think we deserve it.

Maybe it's not the concept that we're resistant to; maybe it's the word. When you think of the word "fun" what comes to mind? Carnival rides and parties? Skiing in the Alps and staying up late? Do you consider having fun a waste of time? Do you feel guilty about having fun? Probably.

Get rid of your preconceived notion of what fun is. We don't like the word anyway. Think of things that satisfy you or make you feel good about yourself. It can be something that other people find boring or messy, like balancing your checkbook, changing the oil in your car, replanting begonias, or running 15 miles. Fun is an individual thing. Nobody can do it for you. Nobody can even define it for you.

The act of reframing the word might open up dozens of areas you hadn't thought of as fun but which offer opportunities for self-enhancement and creativity. Challenge your assumptions about what fun is. Think outside the box, outside of your individual circumstances. Do different things come to mind?

Now spend some time and write a short list of activities which you can define as fun for yourself.

1. _____

2. _____

3. _____

4. _____

Do you do one or more of these things every day? If not, why not? What's getting in your way? What do you do instead? What is taking priority?

If you're like most of us, one of your best excuses for not having fun is not enough time; but fun is not a waste of time. It is necessary, healthy, life-enhancing, creative and energizing, and if you don't have time, you'll have to create some.

Take a typical day and outline your time like this:

| | |
|---|---|
| 7:30AM – 8:00AM | Wake up, have breakfast |
| 8:00AM - 8:30AM | Commute to work |
| 8:30AM - 8:45AM | Coffee with colleagues |
| 9:00AM - 5:00PM | WORK |
| 5:00PM - 5:30PM | Commute home |
| 5:30PM - ?? | |

January 2, 1995

# Monday

| | | |
|---|---|---|
| **6** AM | EXAMPLE<br>6:10am  Wake up<br>6:20am  - 6:40am  Breakfast | **1** PM |
| **7** AM | | **2** PM |
| **8** AM | | **3** PM |
| **9** AM | | **4** PM |
| **10** AM | | **5** PM |
| **11** AM | | **6** PM |
| **12** PM | | **7** PM |

8:00pm  Evening Activities:

When you've finished your schedule, analyze it. Do you really need a half-hour for breakfast when you have coffee at the office? Could you get up earlier, go to bed later? Could you combine your errands after work and do them all in one day? Examine your typical weekend schedule. Is there something there that you could re-arrange in order to make time for having fun? Rethink your days and nights. Create one half-hour.

If you have read the section on flexibility, you read that all change creates some sort of loss, and it is clear here that if you are creating a half-hour of free time, you are giving up something: a half-hour of sleep, an extra cup of coffee, making the beds, or watching television. But you are turning that half-hour into something else: thirty minutes of concentration on your creative spirit.

Commit yourself to spending that time having some fun every day for one week. Make that commitment to yourself. You deserve it. After one week, give yourself the option of renewal. One small step at a time.

I, _____, commit to spending one
(*Print your name above*)

half-hour every day for one full week _____

_____
(*Insert your activity of choice.*)

_____
(*And sign your name here*)

Happiness is not something you strive toward. It is a state of mind you choose. When you choose to make the commitment to having fun, you have told yourself that you are worthy of your own time, that you are valuable, deserving and capable of creative things. You have given yourself what you have deserved all along: personal attention.

# QUANTUM LEAP THINKPOINTS

Fun is essential.

Happiness is a state of mind.

Fun promotes creativity.

Nobody can define "fun" for you.

You deserve to have some fun.

# YOUR TURN

Scribble here. Draw a picture of yourself having fun. Make a mess. Use crayons.

Then tear it out and put it up on your bulletin board at work or the door of your refrigerator at home. Whenever you look at it, remember to set aside some time that day to HAVE FUN.

## Point #11

# *TAKE RISKS*

**Y**ou were probably taught to draw inside the lines, follow the rules, and wear a sweater when it's cold. You were probably not encouraged to take risks, and you were probably told to be very, very careful all the time. Unless you were a very lucky kid.

Unfortunately, fear doesn't motivate, it doesn't encourage, it doesn't teach. Fear creates fear: the fear of making a mistake. Then we pull back, we don't take chances, we play it safe. There is no room for creativity.

All too frequently, the play-it-safe mentality becomes deeply ingrained in our behavior. When we are punished for doing it wrong instead of rewarded for trying to do it better, when we are cautioned against possible danger rather than encouraged toward possible victory, we learn to expend our creative energies avoiding trouble and making excuses instead of searching for opportunities and creating solutions.

Every biography I have ever read about famous people, as well as every motivational book in my library, stresses the importance of taking risks - and not necessarily the kind of risk you may think. Hang-gliding and race car driving are risks indeed, but we take dozens of risks in our everyday life. Calculated risks, educated risks, like driving in the rain, cleaning the gutters, and painting the baby's room white. We take a risk when we pull out onto a busy highway, try a new recipe, fix the plumbing under the sink ourselves, or ask our teenage children to tell us the truth. But these are necessary to living a life with purpose.

There are other kinds of risks that bring joy and excitement into our lives: telling someone "I love you," asking the boss for a new assignment, deciding to have a baby, moving to another town, writing a book, or learning to fly an airplane.

Sir Laurence Olivier said that you could never be a great actor unless you are willing to make a total ass of yourself. That's a risk he took so that he could become a powerful, effective actor. You've got to take risks; otherwise, life becomes mundane; it lacks adventure. Living is survival instead of progress.

Life can be an adventure, if we can understand how to orchestrate risk-taking. Adventure and risk go hand-in-hand. Making life meaningful in the home or workplace is closely related to the ability to articulate adventure. Adventure creates relationships, and relationships are what life is about.

One person's adventure can be another's nightmare. If the risk is too great, the adventure becomes disastrous. There needs to be a foundation of security, an understanding of the facts, preparation, tolerance for mistakes, and a buffer of some sort, a margin for error.

Look at what a risk really is. We can divide it into four stages.

1) The idea.
2) The fear.
3) The action.
4) The pay-off.

The idea is exhilarating, thrilling, tantalizing, seductive. Then the fear comes in: the "what-ifs." What if the business fails? What if my friends laugh at me, I lose my job, I don't like it after I buy it? What if I fall down, or my children leave home? What if my mother doesn't approve?

If we can get past the fear, we plunge into action, and the fears are replaced by the absorption of getting the job done. We're too busy to worry. We're blinded by activity; and then, if we persevere, we're rewarded by euphoria, the exhilaration of success, the pay-off. We are rewarded with a feeling of self-satisfaction, and once we've taken the plunge, we strengthen our "risk-muscle." We can do it again.

Getting through the fear stage isn't easy, but there is a process you can learn which will help. Read through these simple steps.

### 1. Imagine the worst-case scenario.

What is the worst that can happen? A few logical, sensible minutes devoted to what is really the worst that can happen may reveal that it isn't so bad. It may simply be an inconvenience or irritation. Perform a reality check. Often the imagination will make up something far worse than reality itself, and by asking the question, you release your hold on your fear and move to action.

An honest evaluation of the worst case scenario may reveal something pretty dreadful, and considering that outcome will help you prepare for it. This tip comes from NASA. Before taking a flight into space, astronauts are asked to imagine their worst fears over and over again. The more the astronauts imagined the worst, the more they desensitized their fear. The fear become familiar and acceptable. If astronauts are not able to accept the possibility of the worst that can happen, they are not allowed to go into space.

If you are prepared to deal with the worst case scenario, you are prepared to take the risk.

### 2. Do your homework.

Sports psychologist Dr. Bruce Ogilvie has worked with Grand Prix race car drivers, mountain climbers and sky-divers; and he came to the conclusion that risk-takers are, in his own words, extremely cautious people. "An extraordinary amount of intelligence goes into preparing for their activities," he says. "They have analyzed every factor that can operate against them."

Risk-takers prepare, they play out every possible outcome, they do their homework. The more you know about the risk, the more you are able to prepare. The more you prepare, the more confident you will become of a successful outcome. And the more confident you become, the better your chances for success.

### 3. Talk about it.

Ask people what they think. Open yourself up to feedback. This can be tricky, because people will have a tendency to advise you about how to do it - or worse yet, tell you not to do it at all. You need to be open to what they have to say, but remember that their opinion is only an opinion. Don't let yourself be manipulated. The purpose of feedback is to allow you to see as many different points of view as possible before you make your own decision.

### 4. Seek support.

Find those people who will hold you up when you need courage. You want to find those people who genuinely care about your efforts. Support encourages you to live up to your own sense of your highest potential.

### 5. Take one small step at a time.

Baby steps can get you up the mountain. One of the keys to successful risk-taking is understanding that you don't have to do it all at once. Focusing on the end result can be terrifying and fear can get in the way.

Whenever you start something new, whether it's building customer satisfaction, climbing a mountain, or raising a child, always search out one thing that you are reasonably sure of accomplishing and do that first. Successful baby-steps build your confidence, increase your commitment, and most importantly, move you to action.

Think of something you have wanted to do, but which you have always considered risky. It could be personal: a new hobby, an adventure, a trip overseas. Or professional: asking for a raise, changing occupations, applying for a freelance assignment. It could be spiritual or life-enhacing, like going back to school or spending the summer at an ashram.

My Own Risk: _____

Now go through the steps outlined above.

1. What's the worst that can happen if you take this risk?

_____

_____

2. What preparation is necessary to prevent the chance of failure?

_____

_____

_____

3. With whom can you talk about it?

_____

_____

4. Who would listen, offer suggestions and advice without being overly negative? Who could be your support system?

_____

_____

_____

5. What is the first step toward taking your risk?

_____

What is the next baby step?

_____

We are born risk-takers. We could never have learned to walk or ride a bike unless we were prepared to skin our knees a few times. You can't learn anything without taking a risk, and you can't grow up without falling down. We all did it as children. We learn more and faster in the first five years of our lives than we ever do in our entire lifetime. Of course, we had not yet learned to be afraid.

Children explore the unknown and untried. There is no such thing as impossible. They can fly off garage roofs, journey to far-away lands, and eat seven or eight scoops of vanilla ice cream in one sitting. They make mistake after mistake, shake it off and give it another try. Watch children. We can relearn a lot.

Not taking risks is far more dangerous than taking them. Recent medical studies show that the excitement of change and adventure actually slows down the mental and physical aging process. Without risks, we are hopeless and trapped. We have fewer choices. You can see the result of hopelessness in your body and feel it in your soul. You become depressed. You burn out. Risk-taking, on the other hand, promotes vibrancy, energy and good health.

Now go back and look at the risk you chose to examine. What is the best-case scenario? What could happen if your risk turned out to be a smashing success?

_____

_____

_____

Are you willing to have that happen?

     YES       NO

Taking risks, stretching to be all that you can be is fun. You learn; you grow. Your days become more rewarding, vital and fulfilling. You can walk on fire.

# QUANTUM LEAP THINKPOINTS

Risk is necessary.

The imagination can make up something
worse than reality.

Risk-takers prepare.

Adventure and risk go hand-in-hand.

Not taking risks is more dangerous than taking them.

We are born risk-takers.

# YOUR TURN

Go back to the risk you wrote down on Page 112 and get serious. No doubt you have imagined the worst case scenario over and over, but have you spent the same amount of time imagining success?

Talking about things makes them real. Choose one of the people you named in Questions 3 or 4 on Page 112 and call him or her. Make a date for coffee, or just spend some time on the phone. Talk about your risk. Make it real. And document it here.

Who I called: _____

When (date and time!):_____

What was that person's reaction to your risk?

_____

_____

_____

_____

Tomorrow, do the same thing, but call the next person on your list.

Who I called: _____

When (date and time): _____

What that person said:

_____

_____

_____

_____

# Point #12

# *TRUST*

**trust:** n.1. reliance on the integrity, strength, ability, surety of a person or thing; confidence.

2. confident expectations of something; hope.

**faith:** n. 1. confidence or trust in a person or thing; faith in another's ability.

2. belief which is not based on proof.

*—Random House Dictionary*

**T**rust, like its sister faith, cannot be ordered up by will power. It takes a leap beyond logic and borders on the spiritual. Trust is similar to love. It's a way of being as opposed to specific acts, and most perplexing of all, like love, most people find it very hard to do.

I almost chose to delete it as one of Quantum Leap Thinking's 14 points because I am not sure how trust can be taught to adults. We learn about trust very early on. When a parent is abusive, inconsistent, unaffectionate or emotionally dysfunctional, the odds are very high that the child will never learn to trust. When we expect to be disappointed, our expectations guide us in that direction. Unconsciously, we need to validate our fears. The world becomes as we believe it to be.

David Viscott, M.D. writes in RISKING:

> ... the world such children later encounter is in part shaped by their early experiences and expectations. Each new experience

or rejection reinforces the child's belief that the world is a rejecting and ungiving place where he must either endure pain or hide from it and never trust anyone. Since love is based on trust, such a child finds it difficult to risk anything later on in life that has to do with love. Since he fears he will have to endure pain anyway, why should he stick his neck out and only invite trouble? These children often become adults with one overbearing need: to limit any potential loss of love in their lives...

One of the greatest metaphors for trust I have ever experienced is called a "trust fall." You stand backwards on the edge of a wall about seven feet high, the heels of your shoes against the very edge. Below you on the ground are eight and ten people facing each other, four or five on each side. They have locked their arms securely together, forming a net in which to catch you when you fall; but you can't see them because you're facing the other way.

The instructor signals you when they're ready. and you, without looking, are expected to fall backward into the arms of your new support system. You are expected to trust that these people will catch you. In the few seconds you take to decide, you are totally alone. You are worried about your safety. What if they don't catch you? You gather up your courage, take a leap of faith, and fall back, landing in the arms of the people you decided to trust, your new power group.

Some people find it easy to just close their eyes and fall back into waiting arms, some need incredible encouragement and reassurance; but at the moment you feel their arms around you, you experience the excitement, exhilaration, and sense of fulfillment from having taken the risk. Some burst into tears. Although you couldn't see them, you realize that your support system was there for you the whole time. You are sorry that you ever doubted them. The trust fall reflects the process and feelings associated with placing ordinary trust in the people with whom you live and work. It is a proactive process, especially if you have to break through your own fears about trust. You have to make a conscious decision, take action and follow through, just like you would on the edge of the wall of the trust fall.

Whom do you trust?

1. _____

2. _____

3. _____

The people who came to mind are probably people you have good relationships with, because trust builds strong partnerships.

Now think about people with whom you need to build trust.

1. _____

2. _____

3. _____

When you think about trusting these people, how do you feel? If you feel fearful, take some time to examine that fear.

    a. How would your actions be different if you did trust these people?

    b. Acting as if you trusted(_____),

                               *Fill in the name.*

       what specific actions would you take to demonstrate that trust?

    c. What's the worst that can happen if your trust is betrayed?

    d. Are you willing to take that risk?

    e. List specific actions which you are willing to take to demonstrate your trust, i.e., delegate authority or important tasks, give the benefit of the doubt, allow freedom, allow access to privileged information.

_____

_____

_____

Did you include yourself on one of the lists above? Use yourself as a mirror: you will trust others only as much as you trust yourself.

Which of the following statements best describes the way you feel about trusting others?

I won't trust you until you prove to me that you are deserving of my trust.

I will trust you until you prove to me that you are not deserving of my trust.

I don't suggest that you trust everyone all the time. As taking an ill-prepared risk leads to disaster, trusting blindly may well get you in trouble. However, the only way to make a person trustworthy is to trust him or her. Trusting begins with you.

## TRUST THOUGHTS

1. You will only trust if you truly believe that the payoff will be greater than the downside if your trust is misplaced.

2. You will find it easy to trust when you understand, at your deepest level, that the majority of people will become trustworthy when you trust them.

3. You must accept that sometimes, however rarely, others will break the bond of trust.

4. When you trust, it puts the burden on the trusted individual to be accountable.

5. You need to understand the distinction between failure to honor trust as a learning tool and the breaking of trust as a lack of integrity.

6. Trust will grow as relationships deepen. There must be a foundation from which trust can grow.

If you have ever driven down a two-lane highway, you trusted that the driver coming toward you would stay in his lane. You trusted that he could handle his car, that he wasn't asleep at the wheel. If you hadn't trusted that stranger, you would have had to pull over to the side of the road until he passed. If you continued to do that for the whole trip, it would have taken you days to get where you wanted to go. If you ever got there at all.

This is the bottom line about trust: you can't get anywhere without it.

# *QUANTUM LEAP THINKPOINTS*

The world becomes as we believe it to be.

Your support system is already there for you.
All you have to do is ask.

You trust others only as much as you trust yourself.

You can't go anywhere without trust.

# YOUR TURN

Do your consider yourself trusting? Take some time and define what trust means to you.

_____

_____

_____

_____

Where did that definition come from? Did someone teach it to you? You can choose what you want to remain in your belief systems. Write down where you learned what you know about trust and then scratch out the things you want to delete from your internal programming.

_____

_____

_____

_____

You are in control of your thoughts. You can start here creating your own brand of trust. It begins with you.

## Point #13

# *LOVE*

*I* want you to fill in the twenty-five empty squares on the next page with what is listed below:

1. **The five most important relationships of your life.** It doesn't matter if the relationship is current, or even if that person is alive, but you can only put one name in a box and you can only choose five, even if you have six children and wife.

2. **Five plans you have for the future.** The plan may be as short-term as what you are planning to do this evening.

3. **Five material possessions you are attached to.** It can be anything from an old childhood toy to your wedding ring or your house.

4. **Five personal character traits about yourself you consider important.** For example, loyalty, a sense of humor, honesty, or persistence.

5. **Five areas of your life which you hold important.** For example, your health, job, hobbies, your religious affiliation, your social activities.

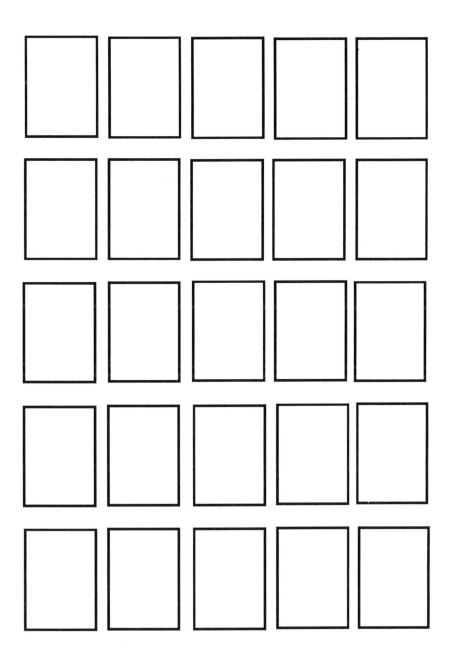

Now you're going to make some choices. You are going to "let go" of all but four of the twenty-five boxes, and you have only 60 seconds in which to do it. If I were with you in person, I would time you with a stopwatch.

Trust your intuition. The whole idea is speed. Don't analyze or think about your choices. Just cross them out as you make your decisions, and when you are done, write the four remaining choices here.

1. _____

2. _____

3. _____

4. _____

Chances are you chose four relationships. Most people do. The exercise was originally developed for hospices to assist the terminally ill focus on what's most important in their lives and to empower them to rethink their priorities as they settle their affairs. Nearly 90% of the patients chose relationships over everything.

Do this exercise with five of six of your friends or family. I'll bet you find the same thing. Most people choose relationships.

Now if that's true, why do we consistently jeopardize relationships for all those things we just crossed out: money, success, hobbies, work, the church, the community, our jewelry and our cars? Why do corporations have trouble implementing customer service programs? Why don't we always act like we love those people we named?

We are all human and will sometimes make choices that hurt or wound. Love involves forgiveness of others for past hurts and forgiveness of ourselves for past mistakes. Forgiveness allows us to be in the present, clear and creative.

List two people, either living or deceased, toward whom you hold anger, resentment, hostility or about whom you feel guilty.

1. _____

2. _____

Can you choose to forgive them? Can you forgive yourself? Perhaps you can begin the healing process by writing a letter saying those things you needed to say and never did. Express your anger, hurt, disappointment and guilt. If one of those letters needs to be addressed to you, write yourself a letter.

Dear _____,

Dear _____,

Now tear the page out and get rid of it. It doesn't matter if you mail it, give it to the person you wrote it to, or throw it away. The important thing is that you removed what was in the way of how you communicated with those people. Now you can start fresh and clean.

Think of love as a filter through which you view the world. Love is a clean filter—clear, unconditional, and true. Love sees the best in others and forgives the worst. With a clear filter, you see that the problem is seldom about others. The problem lies in your filter, the way you see things.

The next time somebody comes at you with anger, switch your mindset. They're coming at you with a cry for help. Clean your filter, change the way you see it, and react with love.

We may have been given some bad lessons in love because it is often used to manipulate. If you get good grades, you will be loved; bad grades, you won't. It's no wonder that so many of us find love confusing. We've been conditioned to love those who are good and do good things, ourselves included. If those expectations are not met, love is threatened or withheld. But this is not love. Love has nothing attached to it. When love becomes conditional, it is only a tool for control.

Look over your choices again and think about how you live. Do you consistently put your focus on that which you said is important? If you chose relationships, do you let those people know you love them? Do you support them and what they value?

Imagine that only two emotions exist: love and fear. Strip down any emotion - jealousy, hate, envy, longing, insecurity, trust - and you will find one or the other at its core: love or fear.

Now, let go of fear.

What's left?

# QUANTUM LEAP THINKPOINTS

Love sees the best in others and forgives the worst.

Love is a way of being, not something you do.

Love is unconditional.

Only two emotions exist: love and fear.
Love is letting go of fear.

# YOUR TURN

It was probably a good exercise to write a letter to people that you needed to forgive, but perhaps a better one is to write a letter to people you love. Maybe they don't even know.

And maybe that letter ought to be addressed to you.

One this page, write another letter expressing your love:

Dear _____,

Point #14

# *SUPPORT*

**C**ancer patients in support groups live 60% longer than the patients in isolation. That's a fact you may find easy to accept when talking about people with terminal diseases, but you probably think that it doesn't apply to your life. After all, you have friends.

But support goes beyond basic friendship. Support provides synergy and ignites energy. Without support, we are disconnected and unempowered. Together, we can provide magic for one another. You can do things you could never do alone. To make a conscious decision to create a support group of your own is one of the most basic of the 14 Points of Quantum Leap Thinking.

"Support group" may sound a little too clinical for you. I like the term Power Group, because support provides power. Whatever you call it, you must take time, care and patience in choosing the people in it. The true power lies in the chemistry of the group. Take notice those who are in harmony with your ideals, your principles, and values.

The people you choose must be willing to persist, explore, listen, give advice, and take positive criticism without being defensive. Above all, they must trust and be trusted. These are the people you can confide in, be vulnerable with, and committed to. These are people who are willing to take risks with you.

A Power Group is a collective mechanism for successful brainstorming and other forms of idea generation, too. It is your brainpower multiplied. A successful Power Group produces its own creative explosion.

Support, however, goes both ways. Giving support is easy. Supporting others answers some little selfish need in ourselves; it makes us feel good about ourselves and look good to others. It gives us control.

But to accept support we have to admit that we need help in the first place and then put ourselves in the vulnerable position of asking for it. It takes courage to do that. We might be turned down.

This is a good place to start when crafting your Power Group. Who can you go to for help?

Which of your family or friends would loan you money?

_____

Who would get up in the middle of the night and drive you to the train station or the hospital?

_____

Who would feed your cat while you go on vacation?

_____

Those are probably three people who should be in your Power Group, if they're not already.

Who would you loan money to?

_____

Who would you drive somewhere in the middle of the night?

_____

Whose cat would you feed?

_____

If you filled in those blanks easily, you have a Power Group already. If you haven't recognized it, this is a source of power and energy you aren't taking advantage of.

Do you have enough support in your life?  YES  NO  MAYBE
Do you give enough support to others?     YES  NO  MAYBE

If you answered YES to both of those questions, you have unlimited strength and spirit. You are capable of personal magic.

# QUANTUM LEAP THINKPOINTS

People live longer with support.

Support provides the power to manage change.

You probably have a Power Group already.

Giving support is easy; accepting support takes courage.

Support creates synergy and personal magic.

# YOUR TURN

Support and partnership are almost interchangeable. You build partnerships; you seek support. And the end result is a source of energy, brainpower and endless possibilities.

You already may take comfort in knowing you have a Power Group, but do you use them?

Write a list of things that your Power Group can help you with. Write the longest list you can. Write 50 things. Then cross out the first 25. Those were the obvious ones. But the last half of your list are probably things you figure you didn't need help with.

Yes, you do.

PART THREE:

# THE MAGIC OF
# QUANTUM LEAP THINKING

Webster's defines the word *quantum* as "... energy regarded as a unit." This is exactly the way I like to think of Quantum Leap Thinking: a unit of powerful, personal energy.

Think about the elements that make up the magic of Quantum Leap Thinking. The foundation upon which everything is balanced is a solid triangle of Quantum Skills:

**Creative Thinking** gives us the ability to make the invisible visible and the impossible possible. Start with just five pieces of advice.

1. Create space.

2. Do something different.

3. Challenge assumptions.

4. Create continuous challenge.

5. Forgive failure.

**Change Management** is as unavoidable as change itself, but we can make change work for us if we take specific action steps:

Be Aware

Accept Compromise

Weigh the Pros and Cons

Make a Contract

Break the Change into Small Steps

Create A Routine

Be Patient

See the Big Picture

Develop a Support System

Be Creative

Communicate

Celebrate

**Continuous Learning** is a trinity of willingness to learn, problem-solving and the process of learning itself, a never-ending circle of idea, test, reflection, question, and contemplation.

Quantum Leap Thinking starts with that sturdy basis for a magical leap and builds 14 points into the equation. The Foundation is always first, but the 14 points can be assimilated into your life in any order. It is the combination that creates the leap, not the sequence.

## THE 14 POINTS OF QUANTUM LEAP THINKING

Pay attention
Turn fear into power
Hold a vision
Enlarge goals
Be flexible
Have commitment
Empower others
Communicate with integrity
Create partnership
Have fun
Take risks
Trust
Love
Support

Build your own foundation for a magical Quantum Leap. You have the information necessary to create your personal unit of Quantum energy.

# AFTERWORD

Self-discovery is the most exciting journey you will ever take. The tools outlined in this workbook can be carried with you and used on an on-going basis for self-reflection and self-renewal.

It is my deepest hope that you will continuously open up unlimited possiblities to enhance the joy in your life.

—*James J. Mapes*

# BIBLIOGRAPHY

Barker, Joel Arthur, Future Edge (Morrow, 1992)

Belasco, Ph.D., James A., Teaching the Elephant to Dance (New York: Crown, 1990)

Block, Peter, The Empowered Manager (Jossey-Bass, 1987)

Connellan, Thomas K., Interpersonal Feedback (Quality Progress)

Conner, Raryl R., Managing at the Speed of Change (New York: Villard, 1993)

Covey, Stephen R., The 7 Habits of Highly Effective People (Fireside, 1990)

de Bono, Edward, Lateral Thinking: Creativity Step by Step (Harper Colophon, 1970)

Denning, Melita, Phillips, Osborne, Creative Visualization (Llewellyn Pub., 1981)

Drucker, Peter F., The New Realities ((New York: Harper & Row, 1989)

Fritz, Robert, The Path of Least Resistance (New York: Fawcell-Columbine, 1989)

Gabor, Andrea, The Man Who Discovered Quality (Times Books/Random House, 1990)

Garfield, Charles, Peak Performers (New York: Morrow, 1986)

Gellerman, Ph.D., Saul W., Motivation in the Real World (Dutton, 1992)

Gershon, David & Straub, Gail, Empowerment: The Art of Creating Your Life the Way You Want It (New York: Delta, 1989)

Givens, Charles J., Super Self (Simon & Schuster, 1993)

Goldway, Elliott m., ed. Inner Balance: The Power of Holistic Healing (Spectrumm 1979)

Handy, Charles, The Age of Unreason (Harvard Business School Press, 1989)

Harman, Ph.D. Willis, Rheingold, Howard, Higher Creativity: Liberating the Unconscious for Breakthrough Insights (Jeremy P. Tarcher, Inc., 1984)

Herbert, Nick, Quantum Reality: Beyond the New Physics (Anchor Press/Doubleday, 1985)

Herman, Stanley M., A Force of Ones (Jossey-Boss, 1994)

Hill, Napoleon, Think and Grow Rich (Fawcett Crest, 1960)

Jampolsky, M.D., Derald G., Love is Letting Go of Fear (Celestial Arts, 1979)

Jeffers, Ph.D., Susan, Feel the Fear and Do it Anyway (Harcourt Brace Jovanovich, 1987)

Katzenbach, Jon R., Smith, Douglas K., The Wisdom of Teams (Harper Business, 1993)

Kohn, Alfie, No Contest (Houghton Mifflin, 1986)

Kriegel, Robert J., If It Ain't Broke ... Break It! (Warner Books, 1991)

Leider, Richard J., The Power of Purpose (New York: Fawcett Gold Medal, 1985)

Leonard, George, Mastery: The Keys to Success and Long-Term Fulfillment (Dutton, 1991)

McNally, David, Even Eagles Need a Push: Learning to Soar in a Changing World (TranForm Press, 1990)

Maltz, M.D., Maxwell, Psycho-Cybernetics (New York: Pocket Books, 1960)

Miller, William C., The Creative Edge: Fostering Innovation Where You Work (Assison-Wesley, 1987)

Nierenberg, Gerald I, The Art of Creative Thinking (Cornerstone, 1982)

Olesen, Erik, _12 Steps to Mastering the Winds of Change_ (New York: Rawson Associates, 1993)

Olson, Robert W., _The Art of Creative Thinking: A Practical Guide_ (Barnes & Noble, 1978)

Ray, Michael, Myers, Rochelle, _Creativity in Business_ (Doubleday & Company, 1986)

Perkins, D.N., _The Mind's Best Work_ (Harvard University Press, 1981)

Poppel, Ernst, _Mindworks: Time and Conscious Experience_ (Harcourt Brace Jovanovich, 1985)

Reddy, W. Brendan with Jamison, Kaleel, ed., (NTL Institute for Applied Behavioral Science, 1988)

Robbins, Anthony, _Awaken the Giant Within_ (New York, Summit, 1991)
Robbins, Anthony, _Unlimited Power: The New Science of Personal Achievement_ (Simon and Schuster, 1986)

Safire, William, Safire, Leonard, _Good Advice_ (New York: Times Books, 1982)

Senge, Peter M., _The Fifth Discipline: The Art and Practice of the Learning Organization_ (New York: Doubleday Currency, 1990)

Snyder, Neil H., Dowd Jr., James J., Houghton, Dianne Morse, _Vision, Values & Courage_ (The Free Press, 1994)

Tracy, Diane, _10 Steps to Empowerment_ (New York: Quill, 1990)

Wellins, Richard S., Byham, William C., Wilson, Jeanne M., _Empowered Teams_ (Jossey-Bass, 1991)

Wells, Valerie, _The Joy of Visualization_ (Chronicle Books, 1990)

Wheatley, Margaret J., _Leadership and the New Science_ (Berrett-Koehler, 1992)

Wold, Fred Alan, _Taking the Quantum Leap: The New Physics for Nonscientists_ (Harper and Row, 1981)

Zohar, Danah, _The Quantum Self_ (New York: William Morrow and Co., 1990)

For further information about James Mapes' series of audio and video tapes, personal workshops, seminars and corporate presentations, you may contact

The Quantum Leap Thinking Organization
195 Sharp Hill Road
Wilton, CT 06897
Phone: 203-762-1200
Fax: 203-762-8959